English Grammar for Students of Italian

The Study Guide for Those Learning Italian

Second edition

Sergio Adorni, *University of Windsor*
Karen Primorac, *University of Michigan*

The Olivia and Hill Press®

ENGLISH GRAMMAR series
edited by Jacqueline Morton

English Grammar for Students of French
English Grammar for Students of Spanish
English Grammar for Students of German
English Grammar for Students of Latin
English Grammar for Students of Russian
English Grammar for Students of Japanese

Gramática española para estudiantes de inglés

Printed in the U.S.A.

Library of Congress Catalog Card Number: 82-80515

ISBN 0-934034-20-6

CONTENTS

TO THE STUDENT

English Grammar for Students of Italian explains the grammatical terms and concepts that you will encounter in your Italian textbook and relates them to English grammar. With straightforward explanations and numerous examples, this handbook compares English and Italian, indicating similarities and differences. Once you have understood the terms and concepts in your own language, it will be easier for you to understand your textbook.

Since *English Grammar for Students of Italian* can be keyed to any elementary textbook, many instructors will assign a specific section as preparation for the study of a given grammatical topic in your Italian textbook. If you use this manual as a self-study guide, you will need to consult the table of contents and index to locate the specific topic you are about to study. Read the relevant pages carefully, making sure that you understand the explanations and the examples. Do the Review provided at the end of each chapter and compare your answers with the Answer Key at the back of the book.

Suggestions for Learning a Language

1. RULES—Make sure you understand each rule before you move on to the next one. Language learning is like building a house; each brick is only as secure as its foundation. After you have read the explanation of the new grammatical rule, memorize one good example or make up an example of your own. This will help you to remember the rules in a concrete way.

2. MEMORY WORK—Memorization plays an important part in language learning. It is easier and more efficient to learn vocabulary and verb endings in the context of complete sentences than it is to learn them in isolation. Work at memorizing for only short periods of time. If you find you are not concentrating on the material, take a break or do a different part of your assignment.

3. VOCABULARY—Write each word on a separate index card, Italian on one side, English on the other. You can draw or paste pictures for some of the objects or actions. Use index cards or pens of different colors. For example, using blue for masculine nouns and red for feminine nouns will help you to remember gender and you might use green for verbs, orange for adjectives, etc. Be sure to make a note of important differences in meaning or usage between English and Italian.

When testing yourself, look at the English (or picture) side of the card and try to remember the Italian equivalent. Say it aloud and make up a short sentence with it. As you progress, shuffle the deck often so that you see the English word out of its usual order.

4. **Daily practice**—Set aside a block of time each day for studying Italian. Try not to get behind. It is almost impossible to catch up because it takes time to absorb the material and to develop the skills.

5. **Active learning strategies**—Attend class regularly and be an energetic participant in the classroom activities. In the classroom or in out-of-class study groups, assume the role of teacher; explain the material and formulate possible test items.

Practice speaking with your classmates, teachers, and Italian friends, whenever you can. Keep a journal in Italian (however simple) and write down what you did and thought that day. While reading and doing written exercises outside of class, say the Italian words and sentences out loud and record your practice. By actively using the language, you will remember words, phrases, and patterns more readily.

6. **Language laboratory**—It is better to work with any of the media-assisted programs for short periods several times during the week rather than to do it all at one long sitting.

7. **Seize the moment**—The main goal in learning Italian is to become functional in the language, that is to be able to read, understand, speak and write it.

Listen to Italian radio programs, watch TV, see movies, read magazines or newspapers which discuss topics of current interest. Take advantage of any opportunity to travel to the many Italian-speaking communities around the world. It is certainly true that language expresses a culture and a way of looking at life; the more you learn of one, the more you learn of the other.

Finally, do not become impatient when your progress seems uneven or slow. Learning a language requires considerable time and effort, all popular advertising notwithstanding! If you invest the necessary time and effort, you will be rewarded by a great sense of accomplishment in comparison to your starting point.

In bocca al lupo!

Sergio Adorni
Karen Primorac

INTRODUCTION

When you learn a foreign language, in this case Italian, you must look at every word in three ways: meaning, class, and use.

1. MEANING—You learn new vocabulary in Italian by associating each new word with its English equivalent.

> The English word *book* has the same meaning as Italian **libro**.

Often two words are the same or very similar in both English and Italian. These words, called **cognates**, are easy to recognize and remember.

English	Italian
intelligent	intelligente
student	studente
to continue	continuare
dentist	dentista

Sometimes knowing one Italian word will help you learn other words derived from it.

> Knowing that **latte** means *milk* should help you understand that **lattaio** means *milkman,* **latteria** means *dairy,* and **latticino** means *dairy product.*

Often, however, either there is no similarity between words in English and Italian, or one Italian word is not derived from another. In this case, you must learn each word as a separate vocabulary item.

> Knowing that *man* is **uomo** will not help you learn that *woman* is **donna.**

In addition, there are times when words in combination will take on a special meaning. For instance, when we say "They threw the book at him" we are not really talking about throwing books, but about someone being severely punished. Such an expression, whose meaning as a whole ("to throw the book") is different from the combined meaning of the individual words ("to throw" and "book"), is called an **idiom.**

It is important that you learn to recognize English idioms so that you do not translate them word-for-word into Italian.

> "To have a good time" is not **avere** *(to have)* + **un buon tempo** *(a good time),* but **divertirsi.**

Similarly, you will have to learn to recognize Italian idioms so as not to translate them word-for-word.

Fare means *to make;* **coda** means *tail.* However **fare la coda** means "to line up."

2. **CLASS**—English and Italian words are grouped in categories called **parts of speech**. We shall consider eight different parts of speech:

noun	verb
pronoun	adverb
adjective	preposition
article	conjunction

Each part of speech follows its own rules. You must learn to identify the part of speech to which an English word belongs in order to choose the correct Italian equivalent and to use it correctly in a sentence.

In your dictionary, the part of speech is always given in italics right after the word entry. For instance, if you look up "student," you will find "student, *n.*" (noun); if you look up "beautiful," you will find "beautiful, *adj.*" (adjective).

Some words, however, may be used in a variety of ways and, therefore, may belong to more than one part of speech.

Look at the word *that* in the following sentences:

That girl is my sister.	**adjective**
That is not true.	**pronoun**
He was *that* smart.	**adverb**
He said *that* he was busy.	**conjunction**

The English word is the same in all four sentences, but in Italian four different words will be used because each *that* belongs to a different part of speech.

3. **USE**—In addition to its classification as to its part of speech, each word has a special **function** or use within a sentence. Determining the function of a word will help you to choose the correct Italian form and to know what rules to apply.

Look at the word *him* in the following sentences:

I don't know *him.*	**direct object**
Have you told *him?*	**indirect object**
Are you going with *him?*	**object of preposition**

The English word is the same in all three sentences, but in Italian three different words will be used because each *him* has a different function.

Careful

As a student of Italian you must learn to recognize both the part of speech and the function of each word within a sentence. This is important because in Italian, unlike English, the form of most words is determined by their relationship to other words in the sentence.

Compare the following sentences in English and Italian.

The small red shoes are under the small white box.

Le piccole **scarpe** rosse sono sotto la piccola **scatola** bianca.

IN ENGLISH

The only word that determines the form of another word in the sentence is *shoes,* which requires *are.* (If the word were *shoe,* we would have to use *is.)*

IN ITALIAN

The word for *shoes* (**scarpe**) determines not only the word for *are* (**sono**) but also the form of the words for *the* (**le**), *little* (**piccole**), and *red* (**rosse**). The word for *box* (**scatola**) affects the words for *the* (**la**), *small* (**piccola**), and *white* (**bianca**). The only word which is not affected is the word for *under,* **sotto.**

Since parts of speech and function are usually determined in the same way in English and Italian, this handbook will show you how to identify them in English. You will then learn to compare English and Italian constructions. This will give you a better understanding of the grammar explanations in your Italian textbook.

1. WHAT IS A NOUN?

A **noun** is a word that can be the name of a person, animal, place, thing, event, or idea.

IN ENGLISH
Let us look at some different types of words which are nouns:

- a person   teacher, boy, Frank, Smith, friend
- an animal   cat, duck, Fido, Bambi, horse
- a place   city, state, library, Rome, Europe
- a thing   book, house, wine, Sunday, Ferrari
- an event or activity   birth, marriage, Thanksgiving, skiing
- an idea or concept   truth, love, peace, happiness, democracy

As you can see, a noun can name something concrete, that is, something which can be seen, touched, heard, smelled or tasted, such as *Frank, music, wine,* or *Ferrari*. Or, a noun can name something abstract, that is, something which cannot be perceived with the senses, such as *truth, peace, democracy,* or *love*.

Nouns that always begin with a capital letter, such as the names of people and places *(Frank, Smith, Rome)*, are called **proper nouns**. Nouns that do not begin with a capital letter *(house, duck, truth)* are called **common nouns**.

To help you to recognize nouns, here is a paragraph where the nouns are in italics:

> *Italy* produces many agricultural, industrial and artistic *items* which are in *demand* throughout the *world*. The *cultivation* of the *grape* and the *olive* is of great *importance* to the Italian *economy* and many *countries* import fine Italian *wines* and *olive*[1] *oil*. Among the many industrial *exports* are *automobiles, typewriters,* sewing *machines* and electrical *appliances*. *Italy* is also famous for its *handicrafts;* among them *leather*[1] goods from *Florence, glassware* from *Venice, coral*[1] *jewelry* from *Naples,* and *ceramics* from *Faenza*. The *achievements* of Italian *artists* and *musicians* have been recognized for *centuries* and the *popularity* of Italian *fashion,* industrial *design* and *movies* extends far beyond the *borders* of the *country*.

---

[1]These are examples of a noun used as an adjective, that is, to describe another noun. See p. 118.

IN ITALIAN

Nouns are identified in the same way as they are in English. The main difference from English is that nouns in Italian have grammatical gender.

Terms Used to Talk About Nouns

GENDER—A noun has gender; that is, it can be classified according to whether it is masculine, feminine, or neuter (see **What is Meant by Gender?**, p. 6).

NUMBER—A noun has number; that is, it can be identified according to whether it is singular or plural (see **What is Meant by Number?**, p. 10).

FUNCTION—A noun can have a variety of functions in a sentence; that is, it can be the subject of the sentence (see **What is a Subject?**, p. 32) or an object (see **What are Objects?**, p. 144).

▼▼▼▼▼▼▼▼▼▼▼▼▼▼▼▼▼REVIEW▼▼▼▼▼▼▼▼▼▼▼▼▼▼▼▼▼

Circle the nouns in the following sentences.

1. The student came into the classroom and asked the teacher a question.

2. My parents visited Sicily last year.

3. Rome, the capital of Italy, is a very cosmopolitan city.

4. The textbook has a photograph of the Colosseum on its cover.

5. Monday is the worst day of the week.

6. His horse ran in the Kentucky Derby.

7. Barbara and Andrew ordered spaghetti at Alfredo's.

8. Her kindness and understanding were known throughout the university.

9. Doctor George cashed a check at the bank at the corner.

10. My friend Bob has a great sense of humor.

2. WHAT IS MEANT BY GENDER?

Gender in the grammatical sense is the classification of a word as masculine, feminine, or neuter.

Gender plays a very small role in English grammar; more parts of speech have gender in Italian than in English.

English	Italian
pronouns	nouns
possessive adjectives	pronouns
	articles
	adjectives

Since each part of speech follows its own rules to indicate gender, you will find gender discussed in the sections dealing with articles and the various types of pronouns and adjectives. In this section we will only look at the gender of nouns.

IN ENGLISH

Nouns themselves do not have grammatical gender, but they may indicate gender based on the biological sex of the person or animal named by them. For instance, gender needs to be taken into consideration when we replace a noun with a pronoun (see **What is a Pronoun?**, p. 34), such as *he /him, she /her,* or *it*. In this case, we choose the form appropriate to the biological gender indicated by the noun we are replacing.

- nouns referring to males indicate the **masculine** gender

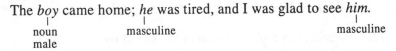
The *boy* came home; *he* was tired, and I was glad to see *him.*
noun   masculine   masculine
male

- nouns referring to females indicate the **feminine** gender

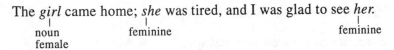
The *girl* came home; *she* was tired, and I was glad to see *her.*
noun   feminine   feminine
female

- all other nouns which do not indicate a biological gender are considered **neuter**

The *city* of Siena is lovely. I visited *it* last spring.
noun   neuter
not male or female

There are a few well-known exceptions, such as *ship,* which is referred to as *she.* It is custom, not logic, that decides.

The S/S United States sailed for Europe. *She* was a beautiful ship.

IN ITALIAN

All nouns—common and proper—have gender; they are either masculine or feminine. The grammatical gender of few nouns is determined by biological gender. Nouns that do not refer to male or female beings have a gender that must be memorized.

The gender of nouns based on **biological gender** is easy to determine. These are nouns whose meaning is always tied to one or the other of the biological sexes, male or female.

males →	masculine	females →	feminine
Paul	Paolo	*Mary*	Maria
little boy	bambino	*little girl*	bambina
brother	fratello	*sister*	sorella
grandfather	nonno	*grandmother*	nonna

All other nouns, common and proper, have a **grammatical gender** that is totally unrelated to biological gender and cannot be logically explained nor easily determined by their meaning.

	masculine		feminine
book	libro	*library*	biblioteca
country	paese	*nation*	nazione
vice	vizio	*virtue*	virtù
Canada	Canada	*Italy*	Italia
Monday	lunedì	*Sunday*	domenica

Remember that it is essential to know the gender of a noun since it determines the gender of all the words related to it (articles, adjectives, pronouns, etc.). When you are not sure, the gender of a noun is always indicated in an Italian dictionary. Also, when learning vocabulary you should memorize the noun together with its article since the article does indicate gender (see **What are Indefinite and Definite Articles?**, p. 13).

Endings Indicating Gender

Gender, whether biological or grammatical, can sometimes be determined by the ending of a noun.

- nouns ending in a consonant → always masculine

il bar	*bar*
lo sport	*sport*
il film	*film*
il weekend	*week*

- nouns ending in **-o** → usually masculine

il libro	*book*
il giorno	*day*
il gatto	*cat*
il maestro	*teacher*

- nouns ending in **-a** → usually feminine

la carta	*paper*
la rosa	*rose*
la casa	*house*
la maestra	*teacher*

- nouns ending in **-i** → usually feminine

l'analisi	*analysis*
la tesi	*thesis*
l'enfasi	*emphasis*

- nouns ending in **-e** → can be masculine or feminine

l'attore [masc.]	*actor*
l'attrice [fem.]	*actress*
il motore [masc.]	*motor*
la lezione [fem.]	*lesson*

As you can see from the above examples, unless we are referring to a masculine or feminine being, the gender of a noun in **-e** is not easily identifiable. There are, however, certain **-e** endings which are more predictable.

- nouns ending in **-ie, -trice, -zione,** or **-dine** → always feminine

la serie	*series*
la motrice	*train engine*
la lezione	*lesson*
la solitudine	*solitude*

There are a few exceptions to the above rules, for instance, **la mano** *(the hand)* is a feminine noun even though it ends in **-o**; **il problema** *(the problem)* is a masculine noun even though it ends in **-a**. Your textbook and instructor will point out additional exceptions.

▼▼▼▼▼▼▼▼▼▼▼▼▼▼▼▼▼REVIEW▼▼▼▼▼▼▼▼▼▼▼▼▼▼▼▼▼

I. The gender of the Italian equivalent of some English nouns is obvious; for others you will need to consult a dictionary. Read the list below and circle M (masculine) or F (feminine) next to the nouns whose gender you can identify. Circle ? next to the nouns whose gender you would have to look up.

Gender in Italian

1. dress	M	F	?
2. car	M	F	?
3. nephew	M	F	?
4. teacher	M	F	?
5. mother	M	F	?
6. shirt	M	F	?
7. bull	M	F	?
8. aunts	M	F	?

II. Indicate whether the following nouns are masculine or feminine.

Gender in Italian

1. luna	M	F
2. autobus	M	F
3. crisi	M	F
4. professore	M	F
5. bocca	M	F
6. azione	M	F
7. teatro	M	F
8. attrice	M	F

3. WHAT IS MEANT BY NUMBER?

Number in the grammatical sense is the designation of a word as singular or plural. When a word refers to one person or thing, it is said to be **singular**; when it refers to more than one, it is called **plural**.

More parts of speech have number in Italian than in English.

English	Italian
nouns	nouns
verbs	verbs
pronouns	pronouns
demonstrative adjectives	adjectives
	articles

Since each part of speech follows its own rules to indicate number, you will find number discussed in the sections dealing with verbs, pronouns, adjectives, and articles. In this section we will only look at the number of nouns.

IN ENGLISH
We indicate the plural of nouns in several ways:

▪ most commonly by adding an "*-s*" or "*-es*" to a singular noun

book	book*s*
kiss	kiss*es*

▪ sometimes by making a spelling change

man	m*e*n
leaf	lea*ves*
child	child*ren*

Some nouns, called **collective nouns**, refer to a group of persons or things, but are considered singular.

A soccer *team has* eleven players.
The *family is* well.
The *crowd was* quiet.

IN ITALIAN
As in English, the plural of a word is usually spelled and pronounced differently from its singular form.

The plural of nouns is formed according to three basic rules.

▪ singular nouns which end in **-o** or **-e** change to **-i** to form the plural

libro	libri	*book*	*books*
ragazzo	ragazzi	*boy*	*boys*
giornale	giornali	*newspaper*	*newspapers*
lezione	lezioni	*lesson*	*lessons*

▪ singular nouns which end in **-a** change to **-e** to form the plural

| casa | case | house | *houses* |
| ragazza | ragazze | girl | *girls* |

▪ singular nouns which end in a vowel with a written accent, an **-i**, or a consonant do not change to form the plural

città	città	*city*	*cities*
virtù	virtù	*virtue*	*virtues*
analisi	analisi	*analysis*	*analyses*
tesi	tesi	*thesis*	*theses*
bar	bar	*bar*	*bars*
film	film	*film*	*films*

Your textbook will point out exceptions to these basic rules.

As in English, collective nouns refer to a group of persons or things, and are considered singular.

La **squadra** di calcio ha undici giocatori.
*The soccer **team** has eleven players.*

La **famiglia** sta bene.
*The **family** is well.*

La **folla** era calma.
*The **crowd** was quiet.*

Careful

A few nouns change gender when they become plural, for example: **l'uovo** (m.) → **le uova** (f.) *(egg → eggs);* **il braccio** (m.) → **le braccia** (f.) *(arm → arms).*

▼▼▼▼▼▼▼▼▼▼▼▼▼▼▼▼REVIEW▼▼▼▼▼▼▼▼▼▼▼▼▼▼▼▼

I. Consider the following English nouns. Circle S if the word is singular and P if the word is plural.

1. teeth	S	P	
2. family	S	P	
3. mice	S	P	
4. cats	S	P	
5. animals	S	P	
6. hair	S	P	
7. dress	S	P	
8. churches	S	P	

II. Consider the following Italian nouns. Circle S if the word is singular, P if the word is plural, or ? if it could be singular or plural.

1. caffè	S	P	?
2. vino	S	P	?
3. penna	S	P	?
4. sport	S	P	?
5. studenti	S	P	?
6. crisi	S	P	?
7. ragione	S	P	?
8. università	S	P	?

4. WHAT ARE INDEFINITE AND DEFINITE ARTICLES?

An **article** is a word placed before a noun to indicate whether the noun refers to an unspecified person, animal, place, thing, event, idea or to a particular person, animal, etc. (see **What is a Noun?**, p. 4).

> I saw *a* boy in the street.
> |
> an unspecified boy

> I saw *the* boy you spoke about.
> |
> a particular boy

Indefinite Articles

IN ENGLISH
An **indefinite article** is used before a noun when we are not speaking of a particular person, animal, etc. There are two indefinite articles, *a* and *an*.

A is used before a word beginning with a consonant.

> I saw *a* boy in the street.
> |
> not a particular boy

An is used before a word beginning with a vowel.

> We visited *an* island in the Adriatic.
> |
> not a particular island

The indefinite article is used only with a singular noun. With a plural noun, the word *some* may be used in place of the indefinite article, but it is usually omitted (see **What is Meant by Number?**, p. 10).

> I saw boys in the street.
> I saw *some* boys in the street.

> I visited islands in the Adriatic.
> I visited *some* islands in the Adriatic.

IN ITALIAN
As in English, an indefinite article is used before a noun when it refers to an unspecified person, animal, etc. In Italian, however, the indefinite article has different forms because it must match the gender of the noun it modifies. In order to select the proper form, you must consider

whether the noun is masculine or feminine (see **What is Meant by Gender?**, p. 6). This "matching" is called **agreement** (one says that "the article *agrees* with the noun").

- **un** precedes a masculine singular noun

  > **un** libro   *a book*
  > **un** ragazzo   *a boy*

- **uno** precedes a masculine singular noun which begins with a **z-** or an **s + consonant-**

  > **uno** zio   *an uncle*
  > **uno** studente   *a student*

- **una** precedes a feminine singular noun

  > **una** casa   *a house*
  > **una** ragazza   *a girl*

- **un'** precedes a feminine singular noun which begins with a vowel

  > **un'** automobile   *an automobile*
  > **un'** amica   *a girl friend*

The indefinite article is used only with a singular noun; if the noun is plural, the partitive usually replaces it (see **What is a Partitive?**, p. 18).

Definite Articles

IN ENGLISH

A **definite article** is used before a noun when we are speaking about a particular person, animal, place, thing, event, or idea. There is one definite article, ***the***.

> I saw *the* boy you spoke about.
> |
>   a particular boy

> We visited *the* island you recommended.
> |
>   a particular island

The definite article remains *the* when the noun becomes plural.

> I saw *the* boys you spoke about.
> We visited *the* islands you recommended.

IN ITALIAN

As in English, a definite article is used before a noun when referring to a particular person, animal, etc. In Italian, however, the definite article has different forms because it must match the gender and number of the noun it modifies. In order to select the proper form, you must consider whether the noun is masculine or feminine, singular or plural. This "matching" is called **agreement** (one says that "the article *agrees* with the noun").

- **il** precedes a masculine singular noun

il libro	*the book*
il ragazzo	*the boy*

- **lo** precedes a masculine singular noun which begins with a **z-** or an **s** + consonant-

lo zio	*the uncle*
lo studente	*the student*

- **la** precedes a feminine singular noun

la casa	*the house*
la ragazza	*the girl*

- **l'** precedes a masculine or feminine singular noun which begins with a vowel.

l'anno [masc.]	*the year*
l'orologio [masc.]	*the watch*
l'idea [fem.]	*the idea*
l'alba [fem.]	*the dawn*

- **i** precedes a masculine plural noun

i libri	*the books*
i ragazzi	*the boys*

- **gli** precedes a masculine plural noun which begins with either **z-** or **s** + consonant-, or a vowel

gli studenti	*the students*
gli anni	*the years*

- **le** precedes a feminine plural noun

le case	*the houses*
le ragazze	*the girls*

Here is a chart you can use as reference:

	INDEFINITE ARTICLES		DEFINITE ARTICLES			
	Singular		Singular		Plural	
Noun begins with:	masc.	fem.	masc.	fem.	masc.	fem.
1. vowel	un	un'	l'	l'	gli	le
2. z or s + consonant	uno	una	lo	la	gli	le
3. other consonant	un	una	il	la	i	le

Careful

The definite article is used more frequently in Italian than in English. Compare the following Italian and English sentences.

> **La** guerra è terribile.
> *War is terrible.*

> Quella donna è **la** signora Bianchi.
> *That woman is Mrs. Bianchi.*

> **L'**Italia acoglie bene **i** turisti.
> *Italy welcomes tourists.*

Consult your Italian textbook to learn when to use the definite article in Italian.

▼▼▼▼▼▼▼▼▼▼▼▼▼▼▼▼▼REVIEW▼▼▼▼▼▼▼▼▼▼▼▼▼▼▼▼▼▼

The following is a list of English nouns preceded by definite or indefinite articles. The Italian dictionary entry shows you if the noun (n.) is masculine (m.) or feminine (f.).

■ Write the Italian article for each noun in the space provided.

	Dictionary entry	Italian article
1. **the** books	libro (n.m.)	_____
2. **the** roses	rosa (n.f.)	_____
3. **a** friend	amico (n.m.)	_____
4. **the** uncles	zio (n. m.)	_____
5. **an** apple	mela (n.f.)	_____
6. **a** stadium	stadio (n.m.)	_____
7. **the** years	anno (n.m.)	_____
8. **a** friend	amica (n.f.)	_____
9. **the** string	spago (n.m.)	_____
10. **the** idea	idea (n.f.)	_____

5. WHAT IS A PARTITIVE?

A **partitive** indicates that only part of a whole (*some* bread, *some* water) or part of a group of things or people (*some* letters, *some* boys) is being referred to.

IN ENGLISH
The idea of the partitive is normally expressed with *some* or *any*, although these words are often dropped.

> He is buying (*some*) bread.
> She drank (*some*) water.
> I saw (*some*) boys on the street.
> I don't have (*any*) friends here.

IN ITALIAN
Partitives have a singular and a plural form. They are normally expressed by the word **di** + the definite article which agrees with the gender and number of the noun.

$$
\text{di} + \begin{cases} \text{il} & \rightarrow \text{del} \\ \text{lo} & \rightarrow \text{dello} \\ \text{l'} & \rightarrow \text{dell'} \\ \text{la} & \rightarrow \text{della} \end{cases} \text{singular}
$$

$$
\begin{cases} \text{i} & \rightarrow \text{dei} \\ \text{gli} & \rightarrow \text{degli} \\ \text{le} & \rightarrow \text{delle} \end{cases} \text{plural}
$$

NONCOUNT NOUNS—The singular forms of the partitive are only used with certain nouns called noncount nouns. As the name implies, a noncount noun designates an object that cannot be counted. Therefore, it is always singular. For example, the noun *water* is a noncount noun because it is a noun which cannot be preceded by a number. (You cannot count *one water, two waters,* etc.)

> Compra **del** pane.
> |
>   di + il
> *He is buying (**some**) bread.*

> Ha bevuto **dell'**acqua.
> |
>   di + l'
> *She drank (**some**) water.*

COUNT NOUNS—The plural forms of the partitive are only used with count nouns. Count nouns are people or things which can be counted. For example, the nouns *boy, class, book* can be preceded by a number (*one* boy, *two* boys, etc.).

Ho visto **dei** ragazzi per strada.
    di + i
I saw (some) boys on the street.

Compra **delle** pere.
    di + le
He is buying (some) pears.

Careful

Although the partitive words *some* or *any* may be omitted in English, the partitive is normally used in Italian. It is optional, however, in interrogative sentences (see p. 53) and is never used in negative sentences (see p. 50).

Hai **(del)** pane? No, non ho pane.
Do you have (any) bread? No, I don't have (any)bread.

Hai **(degli)** amici in Italia? No, non ho amici.
Do you have (any) friends in Italy? No, I don't have (any) friends.

▼▼▼▼▼▼▼▼▼▼▼▼▼▼▼▼▼REVIEW▼▼▼▼▼▼▼▼▼▼▼▼▼▼▼▼▼

Identify which nouns are count nouns (C) and which are noncount nouns (N) by circling the appropriate letter.

1. luck   C   N

2. house   C   N

3. money   C   N

4. chair   C   N

5. pen   C   N

6. sugar   C   N

7. weather   C   N

8. student   C   N

9. patience   C   N

10. water   C   N

6. WHAT IS THE POSSESSIVE?

The term **possessive** indicates that one noun owns or possesses another noun (see **What is a Noun?**, p. 4).

The teacher's book is on the desk.
    | |
   noun   noun
possessor possessed

IN ENGLISH

You can show possession in one of two ways:

1. with an apostrophe—In this structure, the noun possessor comes before the noun possessed.

   ▪ a singular common or proper noun possessor adds an apostrophe + "s"

   John*'s* shirt
   |
   singular possessor

   the girl*'s* dress

   ▪ a plural possessor ending with "s" adds an apostrophe

   the girl*s'* father
   |
   plural possessor

   the boy*s'* team

   ▪ a plural possessor not ending with "s" adds an apostrophe + "s"

   the *children's* playground
   |
   plural possessor

   the *men's* team

2. with the word "of"—In this structure, the noun possessed comes before the noun possessor.

   ▪ a singular or plural common noun possessor is preceded by *of the* or *of a*

   the book *of the* professor
   |
   singular common noun possessor

   the branches *of a* tree

■ a proper noun possessor is preceded by *of*

the dress *of* Mary
|
proper noun possessor

IN ITALIAN

There is only one way to express possession and that is by using the equivalent of the "of" construction. The apostrophe structure does not exist.

To express possession only the following structure can be used: the noun possessed + **di** *(of)* + (definite article) + the noun possessor. (To see how **di** combines with definite articles see p. 18.)

John*'s* shirt   →   *the shirt **of** John*
                                    la camicia **di** Giovanni

the girl*'s* dress   →   *the dress **of the** girl*
                                    il vestito **della** ragazza
                                              |
                                            di + la

the boy*'s* shirt   →   *the shirt **of the** boy*
                                    la camicia **del** ragazzo
                                             |
                                           di + il

the girl*s'* father   →   *the father **of the** girls*
                                    il padre **delle** ragazze
                                             |
                                           di + le

the boy*s'* team   →   *the team **of the** boys*
                                    la squadra **dei** ragazzi
                                             |
                                           di + i

▼▼▼▼▼▼▼▼▼▼▼▼▼▼▼▼REVIEW▼▼▼▼▼▼▼▼▼▼▼▼▼▼▼▼

The following are possessives using the apostrophe. Write the alternate English structure which is the word-for-word equivalent of the Italian structure.

1. Dante's poetry _____

2. the students' notebook _____

3. the girl's bicycle _____

4. Mario's boots _____

5. the children's book _____

7. WHAT IS A VERB?

A **verb** is a word that indicates a physical or mental activity or condition.

IN ENGLISH
Let us look at different types of words which are verbs:

- a physical activity   to run, to talk, to walk
- a mental activity   to hope, to dream, to think
- a condition   to be, to seem, to have

To help you learn to recognize verbs, here is a paragraph where the verbs are in italics:

> The three students *entered* the restaurant, *selected* a table, *hung* up their coats and *sat* down. They *looked* at the menu and *asked* the waitress what she *recommended*. She *advised* the daily special, beef stew. It *was* not expensive. They *chose* a bottle of red wine and *ordered* a salad. The service *was* slow, but the food *tasted* excellent. Good cooking, they *decided, takes* time. They *ordered* pastry for dessert and *finished* the meal with coffee.

The verb is one of the most important words in a sentence. You cannot write a **complete sentence** (i.e., express a complete thought) without a verb. It is important that you learn to identify verbs because the function of many words in a sentence often depends on their relationship to the verb. For instance, the subject of a sentence performs the action of the verb and the object receives the action of the verb (see **What is a Subject?**, p. 32 and **What are Objects?**, p. 144).

IN ITALIAN
Verbs are identified the same way that they are in English.

Terms Used to Talk About Verbs

INFINITIVE—The dictionary form, i.e, the name of the verb, is called an infinitive: *to eat, to sleep, to drink* (see **What is an Infinitive?**, p. 26).

CONJUGATION—A verb is conjugated or changes its form to reflect the subject, tense, mood: *I do, he does, we did* (see **What is a Verb Conjugation?**, p. 42).

TENSE—A verb indicates tense, that is the time (present, past, or future) of the action: *I am, I was, I will be* (see **What is Meant by Tense?**, p. 59).

MOOD—A verb shows mood, that is, the speakers' attitude toward what they are saying (see **What is Meant by Mood?**, p. 57).

VOICE—A verb shows voice, that is, the relation between the subject and the action of the verb (see **What is Meant by Active and Passive Voice?**, p. 111).

AUXILIARY VERB—A verb used to form tenses of another verb (see **What are Auxiliary Verbs?**, p. 29).

PARTICIPLE—A verb form often used with an auxiliary verb to form a tense (see **What is a Participle?**, p. 70).

TRANSITIVE OR INTRANSITIVE—A verb can be classified as transitive or intransitive depending on whether or not the verb can take a direct object (see **What are Objects?**, p. 144).

▼▼▼▼▼▼▼▼▼▼▼▼▼▼▼▼▼REVIEW▼▼▼▼▼▼▼▼▼▼▼▼▼▼▼▼▼

Circle the verbs in the following sentences.

1. The students purchase their lunch at school.

2. Paul and Mary were happy.

3. It was sad to see the little dog struggle to get out of the lake.

4. Paul ate dinner, finished his novel, and then went to bed.

5. Mary suddenly realized that she dreamt every night.

8. WHAT IS AN INFINITIVE?

An **infinitive** is the name of the verb (see **What is a Verb?**, p. 24).

IN ENGLISH

The infinitive is composed of two words: *to* + the dictionary form of the verb *(to speak, to dance)*. By **dictionary form,** we mean the form of the verb that is listed as the entry in the dictionary *(speak, dance)*. The infinitive can never be used as the main verb of a sentence; there must always be a conjugated verb form with it.

> John and Mary want *to dance* together.
>   main verb infinitive

> It started *to rain.*
> main verb   infinitive

> *To learn* is exciting.
> infinitive main verb

The dictionary form alone is used after verbs such as *must, can, will, may, might,* etc.

> Paul must *be* home by noon.
>   dictionary form

> I can *swim.*
>   dictionary form

IN ITALIAN

The infinitive is composed of only one word which ends in **-are, -ere,** or **-ire;** these are called the **infinitive endings.**

> cant**are**   *to sing*
> vend**ere**   *to sell*
> part**ire**   *to leave*

The initial part of the infinitive, called **the stem,** carries the meaning of the word.

> **cant**-are   *to sing*
> sing to

In a sentence the infinitive is used after any conjugated verb other than **essere** *(to be)*, **avere** *(to have)*, or **stare** *(to be)*.

Giovanni e Maria vogliono **ballare** insieme.
  conjugated   infinitive
  verb

*John and Mary want **to dance** together.*

Cominciò a **piovere**.
conjugated infinitive
verb

*It started **to rain**.*

So **nuotare**.
conjugated
verb   infinitive

*I can **swim**.*

Dovresti **studiare** di più.
conjugated   infinitive
verb

*You should **study** more.*

Notice that in the last two examples English uses the dictionary form alone and Italian uses the infinitive.

Careful

When looking up the equivalent of a verb in an English-Italian dictionary, be sure to look for the specific equivalent of the English verb. In English it is possible to change the meaning of a verb by placing short words (prepositions or adverbs) after it. For example, the verb *look* in Column A changes meaning depending on the word that follows.

Column A

to look *for*	I *am looking for* a book. *[to search for]*
to look *after*	I *look after* children. *[to take care of]*
to look *into*	He will *look into* the matter. *[to investigate]*
to look *at*	*Look at* that car. *[to observe]*

In Italian, however, it is not possible to change the meaning of a verb by adding a preposition or adverb. An entirely different verb would be used for each of the various meanings above. When consulting a dictionary, all the examples above under Column A will be found under the dictionary entry *look*, but you will have to search for the expression *look for* or *look after* to find the correct Italian equivalents (**cercare** and **badare**). Don't select the first entry under *look* (**sembrare**) and then add the prepositions **per** *(for)* or **dopo** *(after);* the result would be meaningless in Italian.

to look for	cercare
to look after	badare
to look into	investigare, approfondire
to look at	guardare

▼▼▼▼▼▼▼▼▼▼▼▼▼▼▼▼▼▼REVIEW▼▼▼▼▼▼▼▼▼▼▼▼▼▼▼▼▼▼

I. Under what word would you look up these verbs in the dictionary?

dictionary form

1. Mary *wrote* that book in Italy. _____

2. I *am* tired today. _____

3. The children *spoke* Italian well. _____

4. They *had* a cold. _____

5. He *taught* them everything he *knew.* _____

_____

II. Circle the words that you would replace with an infinitive in Italian.

1. Mary has nothing more to do today.

2. The students must study their lessons.

3. Paul wants to learn Italian.

4. They can leave on Tuesday.

5. Paul and Mary hope to travel this summer.

9. WHAT ARE AUXILIARY VERBS?

A verb is called an **auxiliary verb** or **helping verb** when it helps another verb form one of its tenses. It can also be used alone, in which case it is called the **main verb**.

Mary *is* a writer.	is	**main verb**
Mary *is* writing a novel.	is	**auxiliary verb**
Paul *has* many friends.	has	**main verb**
Paul *has* invited his friends.	has	**auxiliary verb**

A verb tense composed of an auxiliary verb plus a main verb is called a **compound tense**; a verb tense composed of only the main verb is called a **simple tense**.

IN ENGLISH

There are three auxiliary verbs: *to have, to be,* and *to do,* as well as a series of "helping" words which indicate either the tense *(will, would, used to)* or a mood *(may, might)* of the main verb. (See **What is Meant by Tense?**, p. 59 and **What is Meant by Mood?**, p. 57.)

Mary *has* read a book.   **past tense**
auxiliary *to have*

May *used to* read a lot.   **past tense (habitual)**
auxiliary *used to*

Mary *will* read a book.   **future tense**
auxiliary *will*

May the best man win.   **subjunctive mood**
auxiliary *may*

The auxiliary verb *to do* is used to formulate questions and to make sentences negative (see **What are Declarative and Interrogative Sentences?**, p. 53 and **What are Affirmative and Negative Sentences?**, p. 50).

Does Mary read novels?	**interrogative sentence**
Mary *does* not read novels.	**negative sentence**

IN ITALIAN

There are two verbs that can be used as auxiliary verbs **avere** *(to have)* and **essere** *(to be)*. As in English, they are used to form tenses and moods of the main verb (see **What is Meant by Tense?**, p. 59, and **What is a Past Tense?**, p. 76). **Avere** and **essere** are most frequently found as main verbs (see **What are Some Equivalents of "To be"?**, p. 63).

> Il ragazzo **ha** una mela.
>> main verb **avere** *(to have)*
>
> *The boy **has** an apple.*

> Il ragazzo **ha** mangiato la mela.
>> auxiliary verb   main verb
>> **avere**
>
> *The boy **has** eaten an apple.*

> La ragazza **è** al cinema.
>> main verb **essere** *(to be)*
>
> *The girl **is** at the movies.*

> La ragazza **è** andata al cinema.
>> auxiliary verb   main verb
>> **essere**
>
> *The girl **has** gone to the movies.*

Since the auxiliary *do* and its forms *(does, did)* as well as the "helping" words *(will, would, used to, may, might)* do not exist as separate words in Italian, you cannot translate them as such. Their meaning is conveyed by a single conjugated verb form.

▼▼▼▼▼▼▼▼▼▼▼▼▼▼▼▼▼REVIEW▼▼▼▼▼▼▼▼▼▼▼▼▼▼▼▼▼

I. In the following sentences put one line under the auxiliary verb and two under the main verb.

  1. Barb is talking to her mother on the phone.

  2. Did you finish your homework yet?

  3. I haven't seen Tom in about a week.

  4. I would buy a new car but I don't have the money.

  5. Does John still live in Milan?

  6. What were you doing in Rome?

  7. They used to spend every summer in Italy.

  8. Will you call me later?

  9. I may go with them to Sicily.

  10. John might have the money.

II. Circle the English auxiliary verbs that do not have an equivalent in Italian.

  1. They will go to Venice this spring.

  2. Did you write your parents yesterday?

  3. Tom had already graduated from the university.

  4. I would buy a new car, but I don't have the money.

  5. May used to visit us every week.

10. WHAT IS A SUBJECT?

In a sentence the person or thing that performs the action is called the **subject**.[1] When you wish to find the subject of a sentence, always look for the verb first; then ask, *who?* or *what?* before the verb. The answer will be the subject.

John speaks Italian.

QUESTION: *Who* speaks Italian? ANSWER: John
John is the singular subject.

Are John and Mary coming tonight?

QUESTION: *Who* is coming tonight? ANSWER: John and Mary.
John and Mary is the plural subject.

Are the keys on the table?

QUESTION: *What* is on the table? ANSWER: The keys.
The keys is the plural subject.

Train yourself to always ask the question to find the subject. Never assume a word is the subject because it comes first in the sentence. Subjects can be in many different places of a sentence as you can see in the following examples in which the **subject** is in boldface and the *verb* italicized:

Did **the game** *start* on time?
After playing for two hours, **John** *became* exhausted.
Looking in the mirror *was* a little **girl**.

Some sentences have more than one main verb; you have to find the subject of each verb.

The boys *were cooking* while **Mary** *was setting* the table.

Boys is the plural subject of *were cooking*.
Mary is the singular subject of *was setting*.

In English and in Italian it is very important to identify the subject of each verb and then select the verb form which corresponds to that subject. (See **What is a Verb Conjugation?**, p. 42.)

---

[1]The subject performs the action in an active sentence. but is acted upon in a passive sentence (see **What is Meant by Active and Passive Voice?**, p. 111).

▼▼▼▼▼▼▼▼▼▼▼▼▼▼▼▼▼REVIEW▼▼▼▼▼▼▼▼▼▼▼▼▼▼▼▼▼▼

Find the subjects in the following sentences.
- Next to Q, write the question you need to ask to find the subject.
- Next to A, write the answer to the question you just asked.

1. When the bell rang, all the children ran out.

Q: _____

A: _____

Q: _____

A: _____

2. One waiter took the order and another brought the food.

Q: _____

A: _____

Q: _____

A: _____

3. Did the first-year students vote for the class president?

Q: _____

A: _____

4. They say that Italian is a beautiful language.

Q: _____

A: _____

Q: _____

A: _____

5. That assumes I am always right.

Q: _____

A: _____

Q: _____

A: _____

11. WHAT IS A PRONOUN?

A **pronoun** is a word used in place of one or more nouns. It may stand, therefore, for a person, animal, place, thing, event, or idea (see **What is a Noun?**, p. 4).

For instance, instead of repeating the proper noun "Paul" in the following two sentences, it is natural to use a pronoun in the second sentence:

> *Paul* likes to sing. *Paul* goes to practice every day.
> *Paul* likes to sing. *He* goes to practice every day.

A pronoun can only be used to refer to someone or something that has already been mentioned. The noun replaced by the pronoun is called the **antecedent**. In the example above, the noun *Paul* is the antecedent of the pronoun *he*.

IN ENGLISH

There are different types of pronouns. They are studied in separate sections of this handbook. Below we will simply list the most important categories and refer you to the section where they are discussed in detail.

SUBJECT PRONOUNS (see p. 36)

> *I* go.
> *They* read.

DIRECT OBJECT PRONOUNS (see pp. 152, 153)

> Paul loves *her.*
> Jane saw *them* at the theater.

INDIRECT OBJECT PRONOUNS (see pp. 152, 156)

> The boy wrote *me* the letter.
> John gave *us* the book.

OBJECT OF PREPOSITION PRONOUNS (see pp. 152, 158)

> Robert is going to the movies with *us.*
> He did it for *her.*

STRESSED (DISJUNCTIVE) PRONOUNS (see p. 160)

> I saw *her,* not *him.*
> I only sent *them* flowers.

REFLEXIVE PRONOUNS—used with reflexive verbs (see p. 107)

> I cut *myself.*
> We washed *ourselves.*

INTERROGATIVE PRONOUNS—used in questions (see p. 163)

> *Who* is that young man?
> *What* do you want?

DEMONSTRATIVE PRONOUNS—used to point out persons or things (see p. 169)

> *This (one)* is expensive. *That (one)* is cheap.

POSSESSIVE PRONOUNS—used to show possession (see p. 173)

> Whose book is that? *Mine. Yours* is on the table.

RELATIVE PRONOUNS—used to introduce relative subordinate clauses (see p. 175)

> The man *who* came is very nice.
> Mary, *whom* you met, is the president of the company.

IN ITALIAN

Pronouns are identified in the same way as in English. In Italian a pronoun usually agrees in gender and number with its antecedent.

▼▼▼▼▼▼▼▼▼▼▼▼▼▼▼REVIEW▼▼▼▼▼▼▼▼▼▼▼▼▼▼▼▼

The following sentences contain different types of pronouns.
- Circle the pronouns.
- Draw an arrow from the pronoun to its antecedent, or antecedents if there is more than one.

1. Did Mary call Peter? Yes, she called him last night.

2. That coat and dress are elegant but they are expensive.

3. Sofia saw herself in the mirror.

4. Paul and I are very tired. We went out last night.

5. If the book is not on the bed, look under it.

12. WHAT IS A SUBJECT PRONOUN?

A **subject pronoun** is a pronoun used as a subject of a verb (see **What is a Subject?**, p. 32 and **What is a Pronoun?**, p. 34).

> He worked while she read.

> QUESTION: Who worked? ANSWER: He.
> *He* is the subject of the verb *worked*.

> QUESTION: Who read? ANSWER: She.
> *She* is the subject of the verb *read*.

Subject pronouns are classified as follows: the person speaking (the **first person**), the person spoken to (the **second person**), or the person spoken about (the **third person**). These are further divided according to whether one person (singular) or more than one person (plural) is involved. The term **person** in the grammatical sense does not necessarily mean a human being, it can refer to anyone or anything.

Let us compare the subject pronouns of English and Italian.

	ENGLISH	ITALIAN
SINGULAR		
lst person *the person speaking*	I	**io**
2nd person *the person spoken to*	you	{ **tu** [familiar] **Lei** [formal]
3rd person *the person or object spoken about*	he she it	**lui** **lei**
PLURAL		
lst person *the person speaking plus others* *John* and *I* speak Italian. we	we	**noi**
2nd person *the persons spoken to* *Anita* and *you* speak Italian. you	you	{ **voi** [familiar] **Loro** [formal]
3rd person *the persons or objects spoken about* *John* and *Anita* speak Italian. they	they	**loro**

As you can see from the chart, there is not an exact correspondence between English and Italian subject pronouns. Let us look at *it, they* and *you*.

"IT" AND"THEY"
IN ENGLISH
Since a subject pronoun must always be used with every verb form, *it* is used when referring to one thing or idea, and *they* when referring to more than one thing or idea.

> *He* has a new car. *It* is a Ferrari.
> *She* has many records. *They* are all new.

IN ITALIAN
The subject pronouns are used far less frequently than in English (see p. 47). Especially *it* and *they* referring to things are almost never used and should not be translated.

> Giovanni ha una macchina nuova. È una Ferrari.
>> *It* is understood as part of the verb è *(is).*
> *John has a new car. **It is** a Ferrari.*

> Maria ha molti dischi. **Sono** tutti nuovi.
>> *They* is understood as part of the verb **sono** *(ure).*
> *Maria has many records. **They are** all new.*

"YOU" → TU, LEI, VOI, LORO
IN ENGLISH
As you can see from the chart, there are two sets of pronouns for "you." **Tu** and **voi** are called **familiar you**. **Lei** and **Loro** are called **formal you**. To help you learn how to use the correct form, the following section has been devoted to **"What is Meant by Familiar and Formal "You?"**

▼▼▼▼▼▼▼▼▼▼▼▼▼▼▼▼▼REVIEW▼▼▼▼▼▼▼▼▼▼▼▼▼▼▼▼▼

I. In the space provided, fill in the English and Italian subject pronouns that correspond to the person and number indicated.

		SUBJECT PRONOUN	
Person	**Number**	**English**	**Italian**
1. 3rd	pl.	_____	_____
2. 2nd	sing. [familiar]	_____	_____
3. 1st	sing.	_____	_____
4. 2nd	pl. [formal]	_____	_____
5. 1st	pl.	_____	_____
6. 3rd	sing. masc.	_____	_____
7. 2nd	sing. [formal]	_____	_____
8. 2nd	pl. [familiar]	_____	_____
9. 3rd	sing. fem.	_____	_____

II. Write the Italian subject pronoun that you can use to replace the words in italics; if no pronoun may be used, write Ø.

Italian
Subject pronouns

1. *It* is very hot outside. _____

2. *Mario and Carla* are my best friends. _____

3. My keys? I think *they* are on the table. _____

4. Where do your parents live? *They* live in New Jersey. _____

5. *Gloria* is a good student. _____

6. *It* was a good pizza. _____

13. WHAT IS MEANT BY FAMILIAR AND FORMAL "YOU"?

IN ENGLISH

You is the only pronoun of address. It is used when speaking to anyone, a close friend or a stranger. For instance, *you* is appropriate whether you are addressing the President of the United States or a member of your family.

>Do *you* have any questions, Mr. President?
>Johnny, *you* must eat your spinach!

Also, *you* is used whether you are addressing one person or many people. For example, if there are many people standing in a room and you ask: "Are *you* coming with me?" the *you* could be interpreted as an invitation to one person or to more than one.

IN ITALIAN

There are four pronouns equivalent to the English *you:* the **familiar "you"** used with close friends and the **formal "you"** used with persons you do not know well. Each of these has a singular form if you are addressing one person and a plural form if you are addressing more than one.

FAMILIAR "YOU" → TU OR VOI

The familiar forms of *you* are used with members of one's family, friends, children and pets. In general, the familiar *you* is used with persons you call by first name.

1. to address one person (singular) → **tu**

>Maria, **tu** vieni con me?
>*Mary, are you coming with me?*

2. to address more than one person (plural) → **voi**

>Giovanni e Maria, **voi** venite con me?
>*John and Mary, are you coming with me?*

FORMAL "YOU" → LEI OR LORO

The forms of formal *you* are used to address someone you do not know well or to whom you wish to show respect. In general, the formal *you* is used with persons you address with a title: Miss Smith, Mr. Jones, Dr. Anderson, Professor Rossi.

1. to address one person (singular) → **Lei**

>Signor Rossi, **Lei** viene con me?
>*Mr. Rossi, are you coming with me?*

2. to address more than one person (plural) → **Loro**

> Signori Rossi, **Loro** vengono con me?
> *Mr. and Mrs. Rossi, are you coming with me?*

Lei and **Loro**, are always written with a capital letter.

Here are the steps to find the appropriate form of *you*:

1. FAMILIAR OR FORMAL—Is the familiar or formal form appropriate?
2. NUMBER—Is one or more persons being addressed?
3. SELECTION—Select the proper form after completing steps 1 and 2.

Let's find the Italian equivalent for *you* in the following sentences.

> *John, are you coming with me?*
>   1. FAMILIAR OR FORMAL: John → familiar
>   2. NUMBER: one person → singular
>   3. SELECTION: **tu**

Giovanni, **tu** vieni con me?

> *Mario and Gloria, are you coming with me?*
>   1. FAMILIAR OR FORMAL: Mario and Gloria → familiar
>   2. NUMBER: two persons → plural
>   3. SELECTION: **voi**

Mario e Gloria, **voi** venite con me?

> *Mr. President, are you coming with me?*
>   1. FAMILIAR OR FORMAL: Mr. President → formal
>   2. NUMBER: one person → singular
>   3. SELECTION: **Lei**

Signor Presidente, **Lei** viene con me?

> *Mr. and Mrs. Casa, are you coming with me?*
>   1. FAMILIAR OR FORMAL: Mr. and Mrs. Casa → formal
>   2. NUMBER: two persons → plural
>   3. SELECTION: **Loro**

Signori Casa, **Loro** vengono con me?

As you can see, the English question "Are *you* coming with me?" may be expressed in four different ways in Italian and the choice of the appropriate form of "you" has an important social meaning. If you are in doubt regarding the selection of the formal or familiar mode of address, use the formal **Lei, Loro**, since the improper use of the familiar **tu, voi** would be considered rude.

It is also important to note that the selection of the familiar or formal pronoun will determine the form of the verb to be used (see **What is a Verb Conjugation?**, p. 42).

▼▼▼▼▼▼▼▼▼▼▼▼▼▼▼▼▼REVIEW▼▼▼▼▼▼▼▼▼▼▼▼▼▼▼▼▼

Write the appropriate form of *"you"* in Italian.

1. Mr. and Mrs. Verdi, how are you?   _____

2. Angelina, where are you going?   _____

3. Come on children, you must go to bed.   _____

4. Professor Dini, could you explain that again?   _____

5. Daddy, will you play soccer with me?   _____

6. Toni and Piero, what are you doing?   _____

7. Miss Volpe, when are you leaving for Rome?   _____

8. Aunt Maria, can you fix my bicycle?   _____

14. WHAT IS A VERB CONJUGATION?

A **verb conjugation** is a list of the six possible forms of the verb for a particular tense. For every tense, there is a different verb form for each of the six persons used as the subject of the verb. In this section we shall limit ourselves to the present tense (see **What is Meant by Tense?**, p. 59 and **What is a Subject?**, p. 32).

IN ENGLISH
Most verbs change very little. Let us look at the various forms of the verb *to sing* when each of the possible pronouns is the performer of the action.

Singular

1st person	I *sing* with the music.
2nd person	You *sing* with the music.
3rd person	{ He *sings* with the music.
	She *sings* with the music.
	It *sings* with the music.

Plural

1st person	We *sing* with the music.
2nd person	You *sing* with the music.
3rd person	They *sing* with the music.

Conjugating in the present tense is relatively easy because there is only one change in the verb forms: in the 3rd person singular the verb adds an "**-s**".

The English verb that changes the most is the verb *to be* which has three different verb forms in the present: *I am, you are, he, she* or *it is, we are, you are, they are.*

IN ITALIAN
For every tense of a verb, there are six different verb forms corresponding to each of the six persons used as the subject (see p. 36). Learning six forms for every verb would be an endless task. Fortunately, most Italian verbs are regular verbs.

Regular verbs are verbs whose forms follow a regular pattern. Only one example must be memorized and the pattern can then be applied to other verbs of the same group.

Irregular verbs are verbs whose forms do not follow a regular pattern and must be memorized individually.

Subject

Let us now conjugate the verb **cantare** *(to sing)* in the present tense paying special attention to the subject pronoun.

Singular

1st person	**io**	canto
2nd person	**tu**	canti
3rd person	{ **lui** / **lei** / **Lei** }	canta

Plural

1st person	**noi**	cantiamo
2nd person	**voi**	cantate
3rd person	{ **loro** / **Loro** }	cantano

Each subject represents the doer of the action of the verb.

1ST PERSON SINGULAR—The "*I* form" of the verb (the **io** form) is used whenever the person speaking is the doer of the action.

> Generalmente **io canto** molto bene.
> *Normally, **I sing** very well.*

2ND PERSON SINGULAR—The "*you* familiar form" of the verb (the **tu** form) is used whenever the person spoken to (with whom you are on familiar terms) is the doer of the action (see **What is Meant by Familiar and Formal "You"?**, p. 39).

> Giovanni, **tu canti** molto bene.
> *John, **you sing** very well.*

3RD PERSON SINGULAR—The "*he, she, you* formal form" of the verb is used with many possible subjects.

1. the third person singular masculine pronoun **lui** *(he)* and the third person singular feminine pronoun **lei** *(she)*

> **Lui canta** molto bene.
> ***He sings** very well.*

> **Lei canta** molto bene.
> ***She sings** very well.*

2. the singular pronoun **Lei** (formal *you*)

> Signorina Dini, **Lei canta** molto bene.
> *Miss Dini, **you sing** very well.*

3. one proper name

> Maria **canta** molto bene.
> *Mary sings very well.*

4. a singular noun

> Il ragazzo **canta** molto bene.
> *The boy sings very well.*

> L'uccello **canta** molto bene.
> *The bird sings very well.*

The subject pronoun *it* has no equivalent in Italian. *It* as a subject is almost never expressed.

> *John has a Ferrari. **It is** very beautiful.*
> Giovanni ha una Ferrari. **È** molto bella.

> *It* is understood as the subject of the verb **è**.

1ST PERSON PLURAL—The *"we* form" of the verb (the **noi** form) is used whenever "I" (the speaker) is one of the doers of the action; that is, whenever the speaker is included in a plural or multiple subject.

> Io, Isabella, e Gloria **cantiamo** molto bene.
> └─────────────┬─────────────┘
>   noi
> *Isabella, Gloria and I sing very well.*

> In this sentence *Isabel, Gloria and I* could be replaced by the pronoun *we,* so that in Italian you must use the **noi** form of the verb.

2ND PERSON PLURAL—The *"you* familiar plural form" of the verb (the **voi** form) is used when you are speaking to two or more persons with whom you would use **tu** individually.

> Tu, Maria e Susanna **cantate** molto bene.
> └─────────┬─────────┘
>   voi
> *Mary, Susan and you sing very well.*

> In this sentence *Mary and Susan and you* (whom you would address individually with the **tu** form) could be replaced by the pronoun *you* (**voi**), so that in Italian you must use the **voi** form of the verb.

3RD PERSON PLURAL—The *"they* form" of the verb (the **loro** form) is used with many possible subjects.

1. the third person plural pronoun **loro** *(they)*

> **Loro cantano** molto bene.
> *They sing very well.*

2. the plural pronoun **Loro** (formal *you*)

> Signori Casa, **Loro cantano** molto bene.
> *Mr. and Mrs. Casa, you sing very well.*

3. two or more names

> Isabella, Gloria e Roberto **cantano** molto bene.
>   loro
> *Isabella, Gloria and Robert sing very well.*
>
> > In this sentence *Isabel, Gloria and Robert* could be replaced by *they* so that in Italian you must use the **loro** form of the verb.

4. two or more singular nouns

> La ragazza e suo padre **cantano** molto bene.
>   loro
> *The girl and her father sing very well.*
>
> > In this sentence *the girl and her father* could be replaced by *they* so that in Italian you must use the **loro** form of the verb.

5. a plural noun

> Le ragazze **cantano** molto bene.
> *The girls sing very well.*

The subject pronoun *they* referring to things is almost never expressed.

> *Mary has a nice pair of shoes. **They are** from Florence.*
> Maria ha un bel paio di scarpe. **Sono** di Firenze.
>
> > *They* is understood as the subject of the verb **sono**.

Verb Form

Let us again look at the conjugation of the present tense of **cantare** *(to sing)* paying special attention to the forms of the verb. Each of the six persons has a different ending, corresponding to a different subject pronoun. Note, however, that the 3rd person singular form, **canta**, has three possible subject pronouns: **lui** *(he)*, **lei** *(she)*, **Lei** (formal *you*) and the 3rd person plural has two possible subjects pronouns: **loro** *(they)* and **Loro** (formal *you*).

Singular

1st person	io	cant**o**
2nd person	tu	cant**i**

3rd person { lui / lei / Lei } cant**a**

Plural

1st person	noi	cant**iamo**
2nd person	voi	cant**ate**

3rd person { loro / Loro } cant**ano**

The Italian verb is composed of two parts.

1. The **stem** (also called the **root**) is found by dropping the infinitive endings (see **What is an Infinitive?**, p. 26).

Infinitive	Stem
cant**are**	cant-
tem**ere**	tem-
apr**ire**	apr-

The stem usually does not change throughout a conjugation.

2. The **ending** changes for each person and for each tense in the conjugation of regular and irregular verbs. In order to choose the correct endings, you need to know to which group the verb belongs.

Verb Groups

Regular verbs are divided into three groups, also called **conjugations**. The groups are identified according to the infinitive endings.

1st conjugation	2nd conjugation	3rd conjugation
-are	**-ere**	**-ire**

Each of the three verb groups has its own set of endings for each tense. You will need to memorize the forms of only one sample verb from each group in order to conjugate any regular verb belonging to that group. As an example, let us look more closely at regular verbs of the first conjugation, that is, verbs like **cantare** *(to sing)*, **parlare** *(to speak)* or **imparare** *(to learn)* which have the same infinitive ending **-are**. Here are the endings added to the verb stem to form the present tense (see **What is the Present Tense?**, p. 61).

Subject	Ending
io	**-o**
tu	**-i**
lui lei Lei	**-a**
noi	**-iamo**
voi	**-ate**
loro Loro	**-ano**

After you have memorized the endings for a verb such as **cantare**, you can then conjugate any regular **-are** verb by following these steps.

1. CONJUGATION—Identify the conjugation of the verb by its infinitive ending.

   -are or first conjugation

2. STEM—Find the verb stem.

   parl**are** → parl-
   impar**are** → impar-

3. ENDING—Add the ending that agrees with the subject.

Subject	Verb form	Verb form
io	parl**o**	impar**o**
tu	parl**i**	impar**i**
lui lei Lei	parl**a**	impar**a**
noi	parl**iamo**	impar**iamo**
voi	parl**ate**	impar**ate**
loro Loro	parl**ano**	impar**ano**

The endings for regular **-ere** and **-ire** verbs will be different, but the three steps are the same.

Omitting the Subject Pronoun

As you can see, the Italian verb ending indicates the subject. For instance, "parlo" can only have **io** as a subject. Similarly, the subject of "par**li**" can only be **tu,** the subject of "par**liamo**" **noi,** and the subject of "par**late**" **voi.** Since you know the subject from the verb form, the subject pronoun is usually omitted.

par**lo**	*I speak*
par**li**	*you speak*
par**liamo**	*we speak*
par**late**	*you speak*

Subject pronouns are only used to clarify the subject or to add emphasis.

- to clarify the subject in the 3rd person

parla	**lui** parla	*he speaks*
	lei parla	*she speaks*
	Lei parla	*you speak*
parlano	**loro** parlano	*they speak*
	Loro parlano	*you speak*

- to emphasize the subject

io canto	*I sing* [but *he* doesn't]
noi cantiamo	*we sing* [but *they* don't]

▼▼▼▼▼▼▼▼▼▼▼▼▼▼▼▼REVIEW▼▼▼▼▼▼▼▼▼▼▼▼▼▼▼▼

I. This is the regular verb **vedere** *(to see)* conjugated in the present tense.

io	vedo	noi	vediamo
tu	vedi	voi	vedete
lui lei } vede Lei		loro Loro } vedono	

Write the stem: _____

Conjugate the regular verb **scrivere** *(to write)* below.

io _____   noi _____

tu _____   voi _____

lui

lei _____   loro _____

Lei   Loro

II. This is the regular verb **dormire** *(to sleep)* conjugated in the present tense.

io	dormo	noi	dormiamo
tu	dormi	voi	dormite
lui lei } dorme Lei		loro Loro } dormono	

Write the stem: _____

Conjugate the regular verb **partire** *(to leave)* below.

io _____   noi _____

tu _____   voi _____

lui

lei _____   loro _____

Lei   Loro

15. WHAT ARE AFFIRMATIVE AND NEGATIVE SENTENCES?

A sentence can be classified as to whether the information it contains is stated in a positive or negative way.

An **affirmative sentence** states in a positive way the information it contains; it *affirms* the information.

> John works in a factory.
> Italy is a country in Europe.
> They like to travel.

A **negative sentence** does not state in a positive way the information it contains; it *negates* the information.

> John does *not* work in a shoe store.
> Italy is *not* a country in Asia.
> They do *not* like to travel by bus.

IN ENGLISH
An affirmative sentence can become a negative sentence in one of two ways:

1. by adding the word *not* after forms of the verb *to be* and auxiliary verbs such as *can, may, have* (see **What are Auxiliary Verbs?**, p. 29)

Affirmative	→	Negative
John is a student.		John is *not* a student.
Mary can do it.		Mary can*not* do it.
They will travel.		They will *not* travel.

Frequently, *not* is attached to the verb and the letter "o" is replaced by an apostrophe; this new word is called a **contraction.**

> John *isn't* a student.
> |
>   is not

> Mary *can't* do it.
> |
>   cannot

> They *won't* travel
> |
>   will not

Note that the contraction of *will not* is *won't*.

2. by adding the auxiliary verb *do, does*, or *did* + *not* + the dictionary form of the main verb. *Do* or *does* is used for negatives in the present tense and *did* for negatives in the past tense. (See **What is the Present Tense?**, p. 61 and **What is a Past Tense?**, p. 76.)

Affirmative	→	Negative
We study a lot.		We *do not study* a lot.
Julia writes well.		Julia *does not write* well.
The train arrived.		The train *did not arrive*.

Frequently *do, does,* or *did* form a contraction with *not*: *don't, doesn't,* or *didn't.*

A negative sentence can also be formed with negative words such as *no, nobody, nothing, never* (see **What are Positive and Negative Indefinites?**, p. 186).

IN ITALIAN

The basic rule for turning an affirmative sentence into a negative sentence is simpler than in English. You normally place the word **non** in front of the conjugated verb.

Affirmative	→	Negative
Studiamo molto.		**Non** studiamo molto.
We study a lot.		*We **do not** study a lot.*
Giulia scrive bene.		Giulia **non** scrive bene.
Julia writes well.		*Julia **does not** write well.*
Il treno è arrivato.		Il treno **non** è arrivato.
The train arrived.		*The train **did not** arrive.*

As in English, negative sentences can be formed in Italian with negative words such as **nessuno** *(nobody),* **niente** *(nothing),* **mai** *(never).*

Careful

Since there is no equivalent in Italian for the auxiliary forms *do, does* or *did,* you must omit them when forming a negative sentence.

▼▼▼▼▼▼▼▼▼▼▼▼▼▼▼▼▼REVIEW▼▼▼▼▼▼▼▼▼▼▼▼▼▼▼▼▼

Write the negative of each sentence on the line provided.
- Circle the words that indicate the negative in the sentences you have just written.
- Place an "x" over the words that would not appear in the Italian negative sentence.

1. We want to leave class early.

_____

2. He finished his homework.

_____

3. Teresa can spend the summer in Sardinia with us.

_____

4. Robert went to the restaurant with his friends.

_____

5. I am a good student.

_____

16. WHAT ARE DECLARATIVE AND INTERROGATIVE SENTENCES?

A sentence can be classified according to its purpose, that is, whether it makes a statement or asks a question.

A **declarative sentence** is a sentence that is a statement; it *declares* the information.

> Rome is the capital of Italy.

An **interrogative sentence** is a sentence that asks a question.

> Is Rome the capital of Italy?

There are two types of questions based on the type of answer expected.

- **Yes-no questions**—a "yes" or "no" answer is expected.

  > Did you finish the book? Yes, I did.

- **Information questions**—some information is expected. They contain a question word such as *who, what, which, why, when, where* (see **What is an Interrogative Pronoun?**, p. 163 and **What is an Interrogative Adjective?**, p. 131).

  > When will he sing at La Scala? Next fall.

In written language, an interrogative sentence always ends with a question mark.

IN ENGLISH

A declarative sentence can be changed into an interrogative sentence in one of two ways:

1. by adding the auxiliary verb *do, does,* or *did* before the subject and changing the main verb to the dictionary form of the verb (*do* and *does* are used to introduce a question in the present tense and *did* to introduce a question in the past tense—see **What is the Present Tense?**, p. 61 and **What is a Past Tense?**, p. 76).

Declarative	→	Interrogative
The girls *study* together.		*Do* the girls *study* together?
Mark *likes* opera.		*Does* Mark *like* opera?
Frank and June *saw* a movie.		*Did* Frank and June *see* a movie?

2. by inverting or switching the normal word order of subject + verb so that the word order in the question is verb + subject. This is only

used with forms of the verb *to be* and auxiliary verbs such as *will, may, can,* etc.

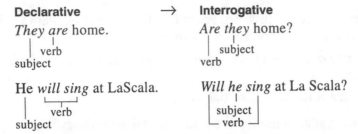

IN ITALIAN
A declarative sentence can be changed into an interrogative sentence by inversion, that is, by placing the subject after the verb.

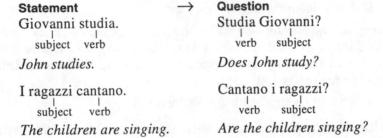

When a statement consists of a subject and verb plus one or two words (the **remainder**), those few words are usually placed between them. The word order of the question is verb + remainder + subject.

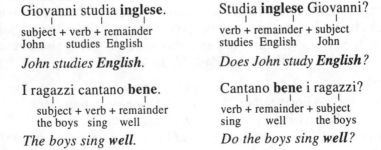

Careful

The verbs *do, does, did* used to form questions in English have no equivalent in Italian and are to be ignored in the formulation of a question.

Tag Questions

In English and in Italian you can also transform a statement into a question by adding a short phrase at the end of the statement. This short phrase is called a **tag** or **tag question**.

IN ENGLISH

The tag question is detemined by the verb used in the statement.

When the statement is affirmative, the tag question is negative.

> John *is* a nice guy, *isn't he?*
> She *had* fun, *didn't she?*

When the statement is negative, the tag question is affirmative.

> John *isn't* a nice guy, *is he?*
> She *didn't* have fun, *did she?*

The end part of the statement *(isn't he, is he)* is the tag or tag question.

IN ITALIAN

The tag is not determined by the verb used in the statement.

When the statement is affirmative, the tag question is formed by adding **vero?**, **è vero?**, **no?**, or **non è vero?**

> Giovanni è un bravo ragazzo, **vero?**
> Giovanni è un bravo ragazzo, **è vero?**
> Giovanni è un bravo ragazzo, **no?**
> Giovanni è un bravo ragazzo, **non è vero?**
> *John is a nice guy, isn't he?*

When the statement is negative, the tag question is formed by adding **vero?**, or **è vero?**

> Giovanni non è un bravo ragazzo, **vero?**
> Giovanni non è un bravo ragazzo, **è vero?**
> *John isn't a nice guy, is he?*

▼▼▼▼▼▼▼▼▼▼▼▼▼▼▼▼▼REVIEW▼▼▼▼▼▼▼▼▼▼▼▼▼▼▼▼▼

The following are declarative sentences.

- Write the interrogative sentence on the line provided.
- Circle the words used to indicate the interrogative in English which would be omitted in the interrogative sentence in Italian.

1. Richard and Kathy studied Italian.

_____

2. Your brother eats a lot.

_____

3. His father can help us.

_____

4. Mark is a friend of his.

_____

5. The girl's parents speak Italian.

_____

17. WHAT IS MEANT BY MOOD?

Verbs can be conjugated in different **moods** which, in turn, are subdivided into one or more tenses (see **What is Meant by Tense?**, p. 59). The word "mood" is a variation of the word *mode* meaning manner or way. The various grammatical moods indicate the attitude of the speaker toward what he or she is saying. For instance, if you are making a statement you use one mood (the indicative), but if you are giving an order you use another (the imperative).

IN ENGLISH

Verbs can be in one of three moods.

INDICATIVE—The indicative mood is used to *indicate* facts. This is the most common mood, and most of the verb forms that you use in everyday conversation belong to the indicative mood.

Robert *studies* Italian.
present indicative

Anita *was* here.
past indicative

They *will arrive* tomorrow.
future indicative

IMPERATIVE—The imperative mood is used to give commands (see **What is the Imperative?**, p. 93). This mood is not divided into tenses.

Robert, *study* Italian now!
Anita, *be* home on time!

SUBJUNCTIVE—The subjunctive is used not to indicate facts, but rather to express an attitude or feeling toward an event. Since this mood stresses feelings about a fact or an idea, it is "subjective" about them (see **What is the Subjunctive?**, p. 97). This mood is not divided into tenses.

They suggested that he *do* it right away.
I wish that Anita *were* with me.

IN ITALIAN

The Italian language identifies four moods: the indicative, the imperative, the subjunctive, and the conditional.

INDICATIVE—As in English, the indicative mood is the most common, and most of the tenses you will learn belong to this mood.

IMPERATIVE—As in English, the imperative mood is used to give commands and it is not divided into tenses.

SUBJUNCTIVE—Unlike English, the subjunctive mood is used very frequently and it is divided into tenses: present, past, imperfect, and past perfect.

CONDITIONAL—Italian grammar also recognizes a mood called the conditional. The conditional mood is used to express the possibility of a result if a certain condition is fulfilled and also to express polite requests. (See **What is the Conditional?**, p. 101.)

18. WHAT IS MEANT BY TENSE?

The **tense** of a verb indicates the time when the action of the verb takes place (at the present time, in the past, or in the future).

I am studying	**present**
I studied	**past**
I will study	**future**

As you can see in the above examples, just by putting the verb in a different tense, and without giving any additional information such as "I am studying *now*," "I studied *yesterday*," or "I will study *tomorrow*," you can indicate when the action of the verb takes place.

Tenses may be classified according to the way they are formed. A **simple tense** consists of only one verb form *(studied)*, while a **compound tense** consists of two or more verb forms *(am studying)*.

Since the indicative mood is the mood most frequently used, we will consider only tenses of the indicative in this section (see **What is Meant by Mood?**, p. 57). The tenses of the other moods will be treated in separate chapters (see **What is the Subjunctive?**, p. 97 and **What is the Conditional?**, p. 101).

IN ENGLISH
Listed below are the main tenses whose equivalents you will encounter in Italian.

Present

I study	**present**
I am studying	**present progressive**

Past

I studied	**simple past**
I have studied	**present perfect**
I was studying	**past progressive**
I had studied	**past perfect**

Future

I will study	**future**
I will have studied	**future perfect**

As you can see, there are only two simple tenses, the present and the simple past. All of the other tenses are compound tenses formed by one or more auxiliary verbs plus the main verb (see **What are Auxiliary Verbs?**, p. 29).

IN ITALIAN

Listed below are the tenses of the indicative mood that you will encounter in Italian.

Present

studio	*I study* *I am studying* *I do study*	present

Past

studiai	*I studied*	simple past
studiavo	*I used to study* *I was studying*	imperfect
ho studiato	*I have studied*	present perfect
avevo studiato	*I had studied*	past pefect

Future

studierò	*I will study*	future
avrò studiato	*I will have studied*	future perfect

As you can see, there are more simple tenses in Italian than in English: present, simple past, imperfect, and future. The others are compound tenses which are formed with the auxiliary verb **avere** *(to have)* + the main verb.

This handbook discusses the formation of the various tenses and their usage in separate sections: **What is the Present Tense?**, p.61; **What is a Past Tense?**, p. 76; **What is the Past Perfect?**, p. 83; **What is the Future Tense?**, p. 86; **What is the Future Perfect?**, p. 90.

Careful

There is often a lack of correspondence between verb tenses in English and Italian. For example, the English present progressive form "I *am studying*" usually corresponds to the Italian simple present tense **studio**. Make sure that you are using the tense appropriate for that language.

19. WHAT IS THE PRESENT TENSE?

The **present tense** indicates that the action is taking place at the present time. It can be:

- when the speaker is speaking   I *see* you.
- a habitual action   He *smokes* when he is nervous.
- a general truth   The sun *rises* every day.

IN ENGLISH
There are three forms of the verb which, although they have slightly different meanings, indicate the present tense.

Mary *studies* in the library.	**present**
Mary *is studying* in the library.	**present progressive**
Mary *does study* in the library.	**present emphatic**

When you answer the following questions, you will automatically choose one of the above forms.

Where does Mary study?
Mary *studies* in the library.

Where is Mary studying?
Mary *is studying* in the library.

Does Mary study in the library?
Yes, Mary *does study* in the library.

IN ITALIAN
The present tense can be used to express the meaning of the English present, present progressive, and present emphatic tenses. In Italian the idea of the present tense is indicated by the ending of the verb (see p. 46).

*Mary **studies** in the library.*
present → **studia**

*Mary **is studying** in the library.*
present progressive → **studia**

*Mary **does study** in the library.*
present emphatic → **studia**

Careful

There is a present progressive tense in Italian, but since it is not used in the same manner as the English present progressive, we have discussed it in a separate section. (See **What are the Progressive Tenses?**, p. 67.)

▼▼▼▼▼▼▼▼▼▼▼▼▼▼▼▼▼▼▼REVIEW▼▼▼▼▼▼▼▼▼▼▼▼▼▼▼▼▼▼▼

Fill in the proper English form of the verb *to read* in the following sentences.
- Write the Italian form for sentences 2 and 3.

1. What does Mary do all day?

   She _____ .   ITALIAN VERB: **legge**

2. Has she read *The Divine Comedy?*

   No, but she _____ it this term.   ITALIAN VERB:_____

3. Does Mary read Italian?

   Yes, she _____ Italian,   ITALIAN VERB: _____

   but not French.

20. WHAT ARE SOME EQUIVALENTS OF "TO BE"?

IN ENGLISH
The verb *to be* is used in a variety of ways:

- for explaining who or what there is or there are in specific places

    There *is* a boy on the street.
    There *are* many drugstores downtown.

- for pointing out someone or something

    There *is* my friend, over there.
    There *are* my books, on the coffee table.

- for telling time

    It *is* 4:00.

- for discussing health

    John *isn't* very well.

- for indicating weather conditions

    It *is* cold today.

- for describing traits and characteristics

    Mary *is* tall and blond.

- for expressing physical sensations or feelings

    I *am* hungry.
    She *is* happy.

- for telling age

    I *am* twenty years old.

IN ITALIAN
In most cases the verb **essere** and the English verb *to be* correspond. However, there are many idiomatic expressions which require the use of another verb or expression.

ENGLISH	ITALIAN
there is, there are	**c'è, ci sono** or **ecco**
to be	⎰ **avere** *(to have)* ⎨ **fare** *(to make, to do)* ⎱ **stare** *(to stay)*

Here are a few rules to help you select the appropriate Italian verb.

"There is, there are" → "C'è, ci sono" or "Ecco"

The English expressions *there is* and *there are* are translated in two different ways depending on their meaning.

- to explain or give the location of something or someone → **c'è** *(there is)*, **ci sono** *(there are)*

    C'è un ragazzo per strada.
    There is a boy on the street.

    Ci sono molte farmacie in centro.
    There are many drugstores downtown.

- to point out something or someone → **ecco** *(there is* or *there are)*

    Ecco il mio amico.
    There is my friend.

    Ecco i miei libri.
    There are my books.

Notice that **ecco** is invariable (it does not change) and that it is not followed by a verb.

Do not confuse **c'è, ci sono** with **ecco**. **C'è, ci sono** are "to describe" and **ecco** is "to point out."

    C'è un nuovo professore d'italiano.
    There is a new Italian professor. [at our school]

    Ecco il nuovo professore d'italiano.
    There is the new Italian professor. [pointing him out]

"To be" → "Avere"

There are some common idiomatic constructions which use the verb *to be* in English and the verb *to have* (**avere**) in Italian. These expressions will have to be memorized. Here are a few examples.

- for expressing many physical sensations or feelings

    I am hungry.
    |
    to be

    Ho fame.
    |
    to have ["I have hunger"]

- for telling age

    I am twenty years old.
       |
      to be

    Ho vent'anni.
      |
    to have ["I have twenty years"]

"To be" → "Fare"

English uses the verb *to be* to indicate weather conditions, and Italian uses the verb **fare** *(to make, to do)*.

    It is cold today.
       |
      to be

    Fa freddo oggi.
      |
    to make ["it makes cold today"]

"To be" → "Stare"

English uses the verb *to be* to discuss health, while Italian uses the verb **stare** *(to stay)*.

    John is not very well.
        |
       to be

    Giovanni non **sta** molto bene.
                    |
    to stay ["John isn't staying very well"]

▼▼▼▼▼▼▼▼▼▼▼▼▼▼▼▼▼▼REVIEW▼▼▼▼▼▼▼▼▼▼▼▼▼▼▼▼▼▼

I. Circle the appropriate Italian translation for the words italicized in the English sentences.

1. *There are* only plastic chairs.   c'è   ci sono   ecco

2. Look! *There is* the train!   c'è   ci sono   ecco

3. *There is* a computer in my office.   c'è   ci sono   ecco

4. *There are* my shoes!   c'è   ci sono   ecco

5. *There is* a book on the desk.   c'è   ci sono   ecco

II. Circle the appropriate Italian verb equivalent of the verb " to be" in the following sentences.

1. Maria *is* thirsty.   avere   fare   stare

2. My father *is* eighty years old.   avere   fare   stare

3. It *is* hot in Palermo.   avere   fare   stare

4. I *am* well, thank you.   avere   fare   stare

5. They *were* very sleepy.   avere   fare   stare

21. WHAT ARE THE PROGRESSIVE TENSES?

The **progressive tenses** are used to emphasize that actions are in progress at a specific moment in time.

> John *is talking* on the phone. [Right now.]
> We *were trying* to start the car. [At that moment.]

IN ENGLISH

The progressive tenses are made up of the auxiliary verb *to be* + the present participle of the main verb (see **What are Auxiliary Verbs?**, p. 29 and **What is a Participle?**, p. 70).

> We *are leaving* right now.
> | |
> | present participle of main verb *to leave*
> present tense of *to be*

> At that moment John *was washing* his car.
> | |
> | present participle of main verb *to wash*
> past tense of *to be*

Notice that it is the tense of the auxiliary verb *to be* that indicates when the action of the main verb takes place.

IN ITALIAN

The progressive tenses are made up of the auxiliary verb **stare** *(to be)* conjugated in the various tenses + the **gerundio**[1] of the main verb. The **gerundio** is formed by adding **-ando** to the stem of **-are** verbs and **-endo** to the stem of **-ere** and **-ire** verbs.

Infinitive	Stem	Gerundio
cant**are**	cant-	cant**ando**
tem**ere**	tem-	tem**endo**
part**ire**	part-	part**endo**

Here we shall be concerned only with the present progressive which is made up of the present tense of **stare** + the **gerundio** of the main verb.

> **Stiamo uscendo** in questo stesso momento.
> | |
> present tense   "gerundio"
> of **stare**   of **uscire** *(to go out)*
> *We are going out right now.*

---

[1]Do not confuse the term **gerundio** which is an Italian verb form with *gerund* which is a verbal noun (see p. 72).

Stai studiando ora?

present tense   "gerundio"
of **stare**   of **studiare** *(to study)*

Are you studying right now?

Present vs. Present Progressive Tense

IN ENGLISH

The present progressive tense is used to describe habitual actions, to state general truths, and to describe an action that is taking place at a specific moment. It is used far more frequently in English than in Italian.

IN ITALIAN

The present progressive tense is used only to emphasize an action that is taking place at a particular moment or to stress the continuity of an action. The present tense, and not the present progressive tense, is used to describe habitual action or to state general truths (see **What is the Present Tense?**, p. 61).

Compare the use of the present tense and present progressive tense in the sentences below.

*John, what **are** you **studying** in school?*

present tense → **studi**

The present tense is used in Italian because you are asking what John is studying in general over a period of time.

*John, what **are** you **studying** now?*

present progressive → **stai studiando**

The present progressive is used in Italian because the word *now* indicates that you want to know what John is studying at this particular time as opposed to all other times.

*Mary, **are** you **working** for the government?*

present tense → **lavori**

The present tense is used in Italian because you are asking where Mary is working in general over a period of time.

*Mary, **are** you **working** right now?*

present progressive → **stai lavorando**

The present progressive is used in Italian because the word *now* indicates that you want to know if Mary is working at this particular time as opposed to all other times.

Careful

Do not use the present progressive to state general truths or habitual actions; use the present tense instead.

▼▼▼▼▼▼▼▼▼▼▼▼▼▼▼▼REVIEW▼▼▼▼▼▼▼▼▼▼▼▼▼▼▼▼

Indicate whether the Italian version of the following English sentences would use the present tense (P) or the present progressive (PG).

1. This semester Robert *is studying* physics.   P   PG

2. Children, why *are* you *making* so much noise?   P   PG

3. I can't come to the phone. I *am getting* ready to go out.   P   PG

4. My brother *is working* for a computer firm in California.   P   PG

5. He *is finishing* an important project right now.   P   PG

22. WHAT IS A PARTICIPLE?

A **participle** is a form of a verb which can be used in one of two ways: with an auxiliary verb to form certain tenses or as an adjective to modify or describe a noun (see **What are Auxiliary Verbs?**, p. 29).

I was *writing* a letter.
auxiliary participle
past tense

The *broken* vase was on the floor.
participle describing *vase*

Participles are found in two tenses: the present participle and the past participle. As you will learn, participles are not always used in the same way in English and Italian.

Present Participle

IN ENGLISH
The present participle is easy to recognize because it is an *-ing* form of the verb: *working, studying, dancing, playing*.

The present participle has two primary uses:

1. as an adjective

This is an *amazing* discovery.
describes the noun *discovery*

2. in verbal functions
   - as the main verb in compound tenses with the auxiliary verb *to be* (see **What are the Progressive Tenses?**, p. 67)

She is *singing*.
present progressive of *to sing*

They were *dancing*.
past progressive of *to dance*

   - in a participial phrase

(By) *studying* hard, Tony learned Italian.
participial phrase

IN ITALIAN
The present participle is formed by adding **-ante** to the stem of **-are** verbs and **-ente** to the stem of **-ere** and **-ire** verbs.

Infinitive	Stem	Present participle
interess**are**	interess-	interess**ante**
sorprend**ere**	sorprend-	sorprend**ente**
segu**ire**	segu-	segu**ente**

The present participle is used mainly as an adjective, in the same way as English.

> Questa è una scoperta **sorprendente**.
> *This is an an amazing discovery.*

"Gerundio"

The two verbal functions (progressive tenses and participial phrases) of the English present participle are expressed in Italian by the **gerundio**.

1. The progressive tenses are made up of the auxiliary verb **stare** + the **gerundio** of the main verb (see **What are the Progressive Tenses?**, p. 67) for a detailed study.

   present progressive
   She is singing.
   present participle

   Sta **cantando**.
   present   "gerundio"
   stare   **cantare**

   past progressive
   They were dancing.
   present participle

   Stavano **ballando**.
   imperfect   "gerundio"
   stare   **ballare**

2. The participial phrase is expressed with the **gerundio** alone; the preposition which is optional in English is not used in Italian.

   participial phrase
   (By) studying hard, Tony learned Italian.
   present participle

Studiando sodo, Tony ha imparato l'italiano.
"gerundio"

Gerund

An English verb form ending in -*ing* is not always a present participle; it can be a verbal noun. A **verbal noun**, also called a **gerund,** is a verb form which functions like a noun.[1]

IN ENGLISH

The verbal noun ends in -*ing* and can function in almost any way a noun can. It can be the subject, direct object, indirect object and an object of a preposition.

Reading can be fun.
noun subject

Mario prefers *reading*.
noun object

Before *leaving,* call me.
noun object of preposition

IN ITALIAN

The English gerund is expressed with the infinitive of the Italian verb.

Reading is fun.
gerund

Leggere è divertente.
infinitive

Mario prefers reading.
gerund

Mario preferisce **leggere.**
infinitive

Before leaving, call me.
gerund

Prima di **partire**, telefonami.
infinitive

---

[1]Do not confuse the term gerund which is an English verbal noun with **gerundio** which is an Italian verb form.

Summary

For reference, here is a chart identifying the various English *-ing* forms and their Italian equivalents.

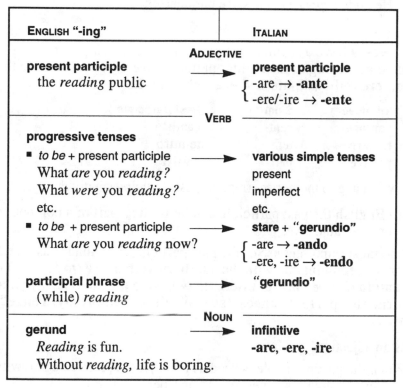

ENGLISH "-ing"	ITALIAN
ADJECTIVE	
present participle the *reading* public ⟶	**present participle** { -are → **-ante** -ere/-ire → **-ente**
VERB	
progressive tenses	
▪ *to be* + present participle ⟶ What *are* you *reading?* What *were* you *reading?* etc.	**various simple tenses** present imperfect etc.
▪ *to be* + present participle ⟶ What *are* you *reading* now?	**stare + "gerundio"** { -are → **-ando** -ere, -ire → **-endo**
participial phrase ⟶ (while) *reading*	**"gerundio"**
NOUN	
gerund ⟶ *Reading* is fun. Without *reading,* life is boring.	**infinitive** **-are, -ere, -ire**

Past Participle

IN ENGLISH

The past participle is formed in several ways. You can always identify it by remembering the form of the verb that follows *I have: I have spoken, I have written, I have walked.*

The past participle has two primary uses:

1. as an adjective

Is the *written* word more important than the *spoken* word?
describes the noun *word*   describes the noun *word*

2. as the main verb in compound tenses with the auxiliary verb *to have*

> I *have written* all that I have to say.
> He *hadn't spoken* to me since our quarrel.

IN ITALIAN

Most verbs have a regular past participle, that is, a past participle formed according to the regular pattern: **-are** verbs add **-ato** to the stem, **-ere** verbs add **-uto**, and **-ire** verbs add **-ito**.

Infinitive	Stem	Past participle
cant**are**	cant-	cant**ato**
tem**ere**	tem-	tem**uto**
part**ire**	part-	part**ito**

You will have to memorize irregular past participles individually.

As in English the past participle can be used as part of a compound verb or as an adjective.

1. The most important use of the past participle in Italian is as a verb form in combination with the auxiliary verb **avere** *(to have)* **: ho cantato** *(I have sung)* or **essere** *(to be):* **sono partita** *(I have left)* to form the perfect tenses (see **What is Meant by Tense?**, p. 59).

2. as an adjective

When the past participle is used as an adjective, it must agree with the noun it modifies in gender and number.

> *the spoken language*
> *Spoken* modifies the noun *language*. Since **la lingua** *(language)* is feminine singular, the word for *spoken* must be feminine singular.

la lingua **parlata**

> *the broken records*
> *Broken* modifies the noun *records*. Since **i dischi** *(records)* is masculine plural, the word for *broken* must be masculine plural.

i dischi **rotti**

▼▼▼▼▼▼▼▼▼▼▼▼▼▼▼▼REVIEW▼▼▼▼▼▼▼▼▼▼▼▼▼▼▼▼

Indicate the proper Italian verb form for the words in italics: "gerundio" (G), past participle (PP) or infinitive (I).

1. At 10:00 p.m. John was *watching* TV.   G   PP   I

2. We had already *gone* when Tom called.   G   PP   I

3. Barbara finished her homework before *going* out.   G   PP   I

4. That antique dealer fixes *broken* dolls and toys.   G   PP   I

5. What are you *doing*?   G   PP   I

6. He likes *playing* tennis.   G   PP   I

7. While *playing* tennis, he sprained his ankle.   G   PP   I

8. He will have *left* by 8:00.   G   PP   I

23. WHAT IS A PAST TENSE?

A **past tense** is used to express an action or circumstances of an action in the past.

IN ENGLISH

There are several verb forms that can be used to refer to the past.

I worked	**simple past**
I did work	**past emphatic**
I have worked	**present perfect**
I was working	**past progressive**
I had worked	**past perfect**

SIMPLE PAST—The simple past is called "simple" because it is a simple tense, i.e., it consists of one word *(worked* in the example above). Regular verbs add **-ed** to the dictionary form to form the simple past: *played, worked.* Irregular verbs are unpredictable; they can be spelled differently: to speak → *spoke*; or they can be pronounced differently *to read* → *read.*

The other past tenses are compound tenses; i.e., they consist of more than one word.

PAST EMPHATIC—The past emphatic is composed of the auxiliary verb *to do* in the past tense *(did)* + the dictionary form of the main verb: *I did work, he did play.*

PRESENT PERFECT—The present perfect is composed of the auxiliary verb *to have* in the present tense + the past participle of the main verb: *I have worked, he has played.* (See **What are Auxiliary Verbs?**, p. 29 and **What is a Participle?**, p. 70.)

PAST PROGRESSIVE—The past progressive is composed of the auxiliary verb *to be* in the past tense + the present participle of the main verb : *I was working, he was playing.* (See **What are the Progressive Tenses?**, p. 67.)

PAST PERFECT—The past perfect is composed of the auxiliary verb *to have* in the past tense + the past participle of the main verb: *I had worked, he had played.* (See **What is the Past Perfect?**, p. 83.)

IN ITALIAN

There are several verb tenses that can be used to refer to the past. Each tense has its own set of endings and its own rules as to when and how to use it. We will here be concerned with the two most frequently used past tenses in Italian: the present perfect and the imperfect.

Present Perfect (passato prossimo)

The present perfect, called **passato prossimo,** is composed of the present tense of the auxiliary verbs **avere** *(to have)* or **essere** *(to be)* + the past participle of the main verb. Although the **passato prossimo** usually corresponds to the simple past in English, sometimes the present perfect or the past emphatic is more appropriate.

Ho giocato nel parco.
auxiliary main
avere   giocare
present   past participle
passato prossimo

I played in the park.
simple past

I have played in the park.
present perfect

I did play in the park.
past emphatic

Sono andato al parco.
auxiliary main
essere   andare
present   past participle
passato prossimo

I went to the park.
simple past

I have gone to the park.
present perfect

I did go to the park.
past emphatic

Selection of the Auxiliary Avere or Essere

Unlike English where the present perfect tense is always formed with the auxiliary verb *to have*, in Italian the **passato prossimo** can be formed with either **avere** or **essere**. You will need, therefore, to know how to determine which auxiliary is required.

Here are some guidelines to help you select the correct auxiliary.

1. All transitive verbs (the verbs which can take a direct object, see p. 145) use the auxiliary **avere**.

2. All reflexive verbs use the auxiliary **essere** (see **What is a Reflexive Verb?**, p. 107).

3. Intransitive verbs (the verbs which do not take a direct object, see p. 145) can use **avere** or **essere** as an auxiliary. Since most intransitive verbs take **avere** as an auxiliary, it is simpler to memorize the relatively short list of verbs which take **essere** and assume the others use **avere**.

Here is a basic list of commonly used "**essere** verbs." The first eight verbs have been grouped together because they can easily be memorized by associating them in pairs of opposites:

andare *(to go)*	≠	venire *(to come)*
arrivare *(to arrive)*	≠	partire *(to leave)*
entrare *(to enter)*	≠	uscire *(to go out)*
morire *(to die)*	≠	nascere *(to be born)*

essere *(to be)*	parere *(to seem)*
avvenire *(to happen)*	piacere *(to like)*
dipendere *(to depend)*	restare *(to stay)*
dispiacere *(to be sorry)*	riuscire *(to succeed)*
diventare *(to become)*	stare *(to stay, to feel)*

A more complete list of the intransitive verbs which take **essere** can be found in the Appendix of your Italian textbook. When you are in doubt about which auxiliary to use, consult an Italian dictionary under the verb infinitive.

Agreement of the Past Participle

The past participle follows different rules of agreement depending on whether the auxiliary verb used is **essere** or **avere**.

1. When the auxiliary verb is **essere**, the past participle agrees in gender and number with the subject of the verb (see **What is a Subject?**, p. 32).

    Paola è **arrivata** dall' Italia.
    subject   past participle
    └ fem. sing.┘

    Paula arrived from Italy.

    Mario è **arrivato** dall' Italia.
    subject   past participle
    └ masc. sing.┘

    Mario arrived from Italy.

    Paola e **sua sorella** sono **arrivate** dall' Italia.
    subjects   past participle
    └——— fem. pl. ———┘

    Paula and her sister arrived from Italy.

2. When the auxiliary verb is **avere**, the past participle agrees in gender and number with the direct object pronoun when it precedes the verb in the sentence (see p. 153). If the direct object comes after the verb, there is no agreement and the past participle remains in the masculine singular form; i.e., the form that is found in the dictionary.

    Quando hai visto Carla? **L'ho vista** ieri.
    direct object   past participle
    refers to *Carla*
    └ fem. sing. ┘

    When did you see Carla? I saw her yesterday.

    Quando hai visto Franco? **L'ho visto** ieri.
    direct object   past participle
    refers to *Franco*
    └ masc. sing.┘

    When did you see Frank? I saw him yesterday.

    Quando hai visto Franco e suo fratello? **Li** ho **visti** ieri.
    direct object   past participle
    refers to *Franco e suo fratello*
    └ masc. pl. ┘

    When did you see Frank and his brother? I saw them yesterday.

Your textbook will go over this rule in detail.

Imperfect (imperfetto)

The **imperfetto** is a simple tense formed in a regular manner by adding a set of endings to the stem of the verb. We refer you to your textbook for the formation of this tense.

There are two English verb forms that indicate that the imperfect should be used in Italian:

1. when the English verb form includes, or could include, the expression *used to*

   I played soccer every afternoon.
      I played could be replaced by *I used to play*; therefore, the Italian equivalent is the imperfect.

   Giocavo a calcio ogni pomeriggio.

2. when the English verb form is in the past progressive, as in *was playing, was studying*

   I was playing soccer in the park.
   Giocavo a calcio nel parco.

In addition, verbs describing physical, mental, and emotional states, as well as age, weather, and time of day in the past are usually put in the **imperfetto.**

   I was very tired, but I was happy.
   Ero molto stanca, ma **ero** felice.

   It was four o'clock.
   Erano le quattro.

Except for the two verb forms listed under 1. and 2. above , the English verb tense will not indicate to you whether you should use the **passato prossimo** or the **imperfetto.**

Selecting the Passato Prossimo **or the** Imperfetto

Both the **passato prossimo** and the **imperfetto** refer to events which occurred in the past. You will have to learn to analyze sentences and their context so that you can decide which of the two tenses is appropriate. As a general guideline, remember the following:

- **passato prossimo** ⟶ tells "what happened"
                         (a specific, completed action)

▪ **imperfetto** ⟶ tells "what one used to do"
(a habitual or repeated action)

tells "what was going on"
(an action in progress)

tells "what things were like"
(description)

Let us consider the sentence "I played in the park." The same form of the verb, namely "played," is used in the English sentences below; however, the tense of the Italian verb **giocare** *(to play)* will be different depending on the question being answered.

▪ "What happened?"

Where *did* you *play* yesterday? I *played* in the park.

In this context, you are asking and answering the question "what happened" at a specific time, i.e., yesterday; therefore the Italian equivalents of the verbs "did play" and "played" would be in the **passato prossimo**.

Dove **hai giocato** ieri? **Ho giocato** nel parco.
⎿___⏌___⏌   ⎿___⏌___⏌
passato prossimo   passato prossimo

▪ "What did you used to do?"

*Where **did** you **play** when you were a child? I **played** in the park.*

In this context, you are asking and answering the question "what did you used to do;" therefore the Italian equivalents of the verbs "did play" (or "used to play") and "played" (or "used to play") would be in the **imperfetto.**

Dove **giocavi** da bambino? **Giocavo** nel parco.
⎹   ⎹
imperfetto   imperfetto

▪ "What was going on?"

Since the **passato prossimo** and the **imperfetto** can indicate actions that took place during the same time period in the past, you will often find the two tenses intermingled in a sentence or a story.

*He **was reading** when I **arrived**.*

Both actions "reading" and "arrived" took place at the same time.
What was going on? He was reading → **imperfetto**
What happened? I arrived → **passato prossimo**

Leggeva quando **sono arrivato**.
⎹   ⎿___⏌___⏌
imperfetto   passato prossimo

Your Italian textbook will give you additional guidelines to help you to select the appropriate past tense. It is useful to analyze paragraphs written in the past tense in English (such as the one below in the Review), indicating whether the **passato prossimo** or the **imperfetto** is needed. Sometimes either tense is possible grammatically, but usually one of the two is more logical or appropriate.

▼▼▼▼▼▼▼▼▼▼▼▼▼▼▼▼▼REVIEW▼▼▼▼▼▼▼▼▼▼▼▼▼▼▼▼▼

Circle the verbs that, in Italian, would be put in the **imperfetto**.
▪ Underline the verbs that, in Italian, would be put in the **passato prossimo**.

Last summer, I went to Italy with my family. Everyone was very

excited when we arrived at the airport. While my mother was

checking the luggage and my father was handling the tickets, my little

sister Mary ran away. My parents dropped everything and tried to

catch her, but she ducked behind the counter. Finally, a manager

grabbed her and brought her back to us. She was crying because she

was sad that she was leaving the dog for two weeks. Everyone com-

forted her and, finally, she went on to the plane with a smile.

24. WHAT IS THE PAST PERFECT?

The **past perfect** tense is used to express an action completed in the past before some other past action or event.

IN ENGLISH

The past perfect is formed with the auxiliary *had* (which is the past tense of the verb *to have*) + the past participle of the main verb.

The past perfect is used when two actions happened at different times in the past and you want to make it clear which of the actions preceded the other.

> She suddenly *remembered* that she *had* not *eaten* yet.
>   past tense   past perfect
>   1   2

> Both action 1 and action 2 occurred in the past, but action 2 preceded action 1. Therefore, action 2 is in the past perfect.

The tense of a verb indicates the time when an action occurs. Therefore, when two verbs in a sentence are in the same tense, we know that the actions took place at the same time. In order to indicate that they took place at different times, different tenses must be used. Look at the following examples:

> The car *was sliding* because it *was raining*.
>   past progressive   past progressive
>   1   2

> Action 1 and action 2 were taking place at the same time.

> The car *was sliding* because it *had rained*.
>   past progressive   past perfect
>   1   2

> Action 2 took place before action 1.

IN ITALIAN

The past perfect, called **trapassato prossimo**, is formed by the imperfect of the auxiliary verb **avere** *(to have)* or **essere** *(to be)* + the past participle of the main verb. The rules for the selection of the appropriate auxiliary and for the agreement of the past participle are the same as for the present perfect (see p. 78).

The past perfect is used to indicate that an action in the past took place before another action in the past, expressed by the present perfect or the imperfect.

Look at this line showing the relationship of tenses.

VERB TENSE:	**Past Perfect**	**Past**	**Present**
	trapassato prossimo	passato prossimo	present
		imperfetto	
	- 2	- 1	0

TIME ACTION TAKES PLACE: 0 → now

- 1 → before 0

- 2 → before -1

Same verb tense → same moment in time

> *The car was sliding because it was raining.*
> La macchina **sbandava** perchè **pioveva**.
>   imperfect   imperfect
>   -1   -1

When both verbs are in the imperfect the two actions were taking place at the same time in the past.

Different verb tense → different moments in time

> *The car was sliding because it had rained.*
> La macchina **sbandava** perchè **aveva piovuto**.
>   imperfect   past perfect
>   -1   -2

The action in the past perfect -2 occurred before the action in the imperfect -1.

Careful

You cannot always rely on English to determine when to use the past perfect. If it is clear which action came first, English usage permits the use of the simple past to describe an action that preceded another.

> *The teacher **wanted** to know who **saw** the student.*
>   simple past   simple past

> *The teacher **wanted** to know who **had seen** the student.*
>   simple past   past perfect

Although the two sentences above mean the same thing and are correct English, only the verb sequence of the second sentence with the past perfect would be correct in Italian.

Il professore **voleva** sapere chi **aveva veduto** lo studente.

imperfetto   trapassato prossimo
-1   -2

> The verb in the past perfect -2 stresses that the action was completed before the action of "wanting to know" -1.

In Italian grammar, the sequence of tenses is more strictly observed than it is in English.

▼▼▼▼▼▼▼▼▼▼▼▼▼▼▼▼▼REVIEW▼▼▼▼▼▼▼▼▼▼▼▼▼▼▼▼▼

Number the verbs or expressions according to the time-line on p. 84.
- Circle the verbs that must be in **trapassato prossimo** in Italian.

1. This morning, Mary *read* the book she *bought* yesterday.

(-___)   (-___)

2. That evening, when she *found* no money in her purse,

(-___)

she *remembered* she *had gone* shopping that morning.

(-___)   (-___)

3. After lunch, Paul *asked* who *had called* him that morning.

(-___)   (-___)

4. This morning Mary *was insisting* that she *tried* to call me ten times.

(-___)   (-___)

25. WHAT IS THE FUTURE TENSE?

The **future tense** indicates that an action will take place in the future.

> We*'ll meet* you tomorrow.

IN ENGLISH
The future tense is a compound tense. It is formed with the auxiliary *will* or *shall* + the main verb. Note that *shall* is used only in the first person singular and plural and only in formal English and British English. *Will* occurs in everyday language.

> Paul and Mary *will do* their work tomorrow.
> I *shall* go out tonight.

In conversation, *shall* and *will* are often shortened to *'ll* : "They*'ll do* it tomorrow," "I*'ll go* out tonight."

IN ITALIAN
You do not need an auxiliary verb to show that the action will take place in the future. The future tense, called **futuro**, is indicated by a simple tense. It is formed with a stem derived from the infinitive + future tense endings.

- **-are** verbs → drop the final **-e** + change **-ar-** to **-er-** + future endings

Infinitive	stem +	Future ending	
parl**are**	parler-	parler**ò**	*I shall (will) speak*
cant**are**	canter-	canter**à**	*she will sing*

- **-ere** and **-ire** verbs → drop the final **-e** + future endings

Infinitive	stem +	Future ending	
tem**ere**	temer-	temer**ò**	*I shall (will) fear*
part**ire**	partir-	partir**à**	*he will leave*

- irregular verbs have irregular future stems + future endings

Infinitive	stem +	Future ending	
andare	andr-	andr**ò**	*I shall (will) go*
avere	avr-	avr**à**	*she will have*

Your textbook will indicate which verbs have irregular stems in the future. Memorize them as the same stem serves to form the conditional (see **What is the Conditional?**, p. 101).

Substitute for the Future Tense

In English and in Italian it is possible to express a future action without using the future tense.

IN ENGLISH
There are two possible substitutes for the future tense.

▪ the present progressive of the main verb (see **What are the Progressive Tenses?**, p. 67)

> We *are leaving* tonight.
> └──────┘
> present progressive *to leave*

▪ the present progressive of *to go* + the infinitive of the main verb

> We *are going to leave* tonight.
> └──────┘ └──────┘
> present   infinitive
> progressive
> *to go*

Both of these constructions have the same meaning as the future tense: "We *shall leave* tonight."

IN ITALIAN
The above progressive constructions are not used. In the spoken language the present tense commonly replaces the future tense to indicate an action about to take place.

> **Partiamo** stasera.
> │
> present
> We **shall leave** tonight.
> └──────┘
> future

> Elena **resta** a casa stasera.
> │
> present
> Helen **will stay** home tonight.
> └──────┘
> future

Careful
While English uses the present tense after expressions such as *as soon as, when,* and *by the time,* which introduce an action that will take place in the future, Italian uses the future tense.

*As soon as he **returns**, I **will call** him.*
            | |
        present   future

Appena **ritornerà**, gli **telefonerò**.
            | |
        future   future

Future of Probability

In addition to expressing an action which will take place in the future, in Italian the future tense can be used to express a probable fact: what the speaker feels is probably true. This is called the **future of probability**.

IN ENGLISH
The idea of probability, what the speaker feels is probably true, is expressed with words such as *must, probably, wonder*.

> I *wonder* who is at the door.
> It is *probably* my mother.
> Charles *must* have it.

IN ITALIAN
It is not necessary to use the words such as *must, probably, wonder*, to express probable facts; the main verb is simply put in the future tense.

*I **wonder** who **is** at the door. It **is probably** my mother.*
              | |
        present tense   present tense

Chi **sarà** alla porta? **Sarà** mia madre.
        | |
    future tense   future tense

*I can't find my book. Charles **must have** it.*
                                      |
                                present tense

Non posso trovare il mio libro. L'**avrà** Carlo.
                                    |
                                future tense

▼▼▼▼▼▼▼▼▼▼▼▼▼▼▼▼REVIEW▼▼▼▼▼▼▼▼▼▼▼▼▼▼▼▼▼▼

I. On the line provided, write the dictionary form of the English verb you would put in the future tense in Italian.

Dictionary form

1. The students will study for the exam.   _____

2. I'll clean my room later.   _____

3. Shall we leave?   _____

4. I won't finish until tomorrow.   _____

5. Will she be here by 9:00?   _____

II. Indicate the tense of the verbs below: present (P), future (F).
■ Indicate the tense the verbs would be in an Italian sentence.

1. As soon as we (1) *finish* our meal, we (2) *'ll leave*.

ENGLISH: (1) P F   (2) P   F

ITALIAN: (1) P F   (2) P   F

2. We (1) *will speak* Italian when we (2) *go* to Italy this summer.

ENGLISH: (1) P F   (2) P   F

ITALIAN: (1) P F   (2) P   F

III. Circle the expression of probability in the following sentences.
■ On the line provided, write the dictionary form of the English verb you would put in the future tense in Italian.

Dictionary form

1. I wonder what time it is.   _____

2. It is probably 3:00.   _____

3. I wonder who has my Italian book.   _____

4. Debbie must know it.   _____

26. WHAT IS THE FUTURE PERFECT?

The **future perfect tense** is used to express an action which will be completed in the future before some other future action or by a specific time.

I *will have finished* my degree by next spring.

IN ENGLISH
The future perfect is formed with the auxiliaries ***will have*** or ***shall have*** + past participle of the main verb: *I shall have taken, he will have gone*. Note that *shall* is used only in formal English and British English.

They will have left before he arrives.
      future perfect   future action
          1   2

Although the verb of action 2 is in the present tense, it refers to a future action (see p. 86). Action 1 is in the future perfect as it will be completed in the future before action 2 takes place.

They will have left by 10:00 P.M.
   future perfect   specific time in the future
      1   2

Action 1 is in the future perfect because it will be completed in the future before a specific time in the future (2).

Observe the sequence of events expressed by the future tenses in the following time-line.

VERB TENSE:	Present	Future Perfect	Future action specific time in the future
	0	1	2
	x	x	x

TIME ACTION TAKES PLACE: 0 → now
                              1 → after 0 and before 2
                              2 → after 1

To use the future perfect (point 1) you have to have an action or event at point 2 with which to relate it.

IN ITALIAN

The future perfect, called the **futuro anteriore,** is formed by using the auxiliary **avere** *(to have)* or **essere** *(to be)* in the future tense + the past participle of the main verb: **avrò preso** *(I will have taken),* **sarà partito** *(he will have gone).*

English and Italian coincide in the use of the future perfect to refer to an action which will have been completed by a future time.

> **Saranno partiti** prima che lui arrivi.
> future perfect   future action
>   1   2
> *They will have left before he arrives.*

> Although the verb of action 2 is in the present subjunctive (in English, it is in the present tense), it refers to a future action. In both English and Italian action 1 is in the future perfect, as it will be completed in the future before action 2.

> **Saranno partiti** entro le dieci.
> future perfect   specific time in the future
>   1   2
> *They will have left by ten o'clock.*

Future Perfect in Dependent Clauses

The most frequent use of the future perfect in Italian, however, is in a dependent clause introduced by a time conjunction such as **dopo che, appena, quando,** etc. This clause refers to an action in the future to be completed before the main action (1), which is expressed in the future tense. Here Italian always requires the use of the future perfect (2), whereas English uses the present perfect (2).

> Stasera **usciremo** dopo che i bambini **avranno mangiato**
>   future (1)   future perfect (2)
> e **saranno andati** a letto.
> future perfect (2)
> *This evening, we **will go out** after the children **have eaten***
>   future (1)   present perfect (2)
> *and **gone** to bed.*
> present perfect (2)

▼▼▼▼▼▼▼▼▼▼▼▼▼▼▼▼▼▼▼▼REVIEW▼▼▼▼▼▼▼▼▼▼▼▼▼▼▼▼▼▼▼▼

Number the verbs or expressions according to the time-line on p. 90.

- Indicate the tense the verb would take in Italian: future (F), future perfect (FP).

1. By *seven* o'clock, we *will have eaten* dinner.

    (___)   (___)

                                        F   FP

2. After they *have visited* Rome, my parents *will fly* to Paris.

        (___)   (___)

              F   FP   F   FP

3. When I *have written* the letter, I *will send* it.

        (___)   (___)

          F   FP   F   FP

27. WHAT IS THE IMPERATIVE?

The **imperative** is the verb form to give a command or to make a suggestion. There are affirmative imperatives (to tell someone to do something) and negative imperatives (to tell someone not to do something).

affirmative imperative	*Open* the door!
negative imperative	*Don't open* the door!

IN ENGLISH

There are two forms of commands, depending on who is being told to do, or not to do, something.

"YOU" COMMAND—When addressing one or more persons the dictionary form of the verb is used.

Affirmative imperative	**Negative imperative**
Answer the phone.	*Don't answer* the phone.
Clean your room.	*Don't clean* your room.

Notice that the subject pronoun "you" is not used. The absence of the pronoun *you* in the sentence indicates that the verb form is an imperative and not a present tense.

You answer the phone.	**present tense**
Answer the phone.	**affirmative imperative**
Don't answer the phone.	**negative imperative**

"WE" COMMAND—When the speaker makes a suggestion that includes himself and others, the phrase "let's" (a contraction of "let us") + the dictionary form of the verb is used.

Affirmative imperative	**Negative imperative**
Let's leave.	*Let's not leave.*
Let's go to the movies.	*Let's not go* to the movies.

IN ITALIAN

As in English, there are affirmative and negative commands.

"You" Command

There are many forms of the *you* command to distinguish familiar and formal as well as affirmative and negative commands (see **What is Meant by Familiar and Formal "You"?**, p. 39).

Here are examples of each form.

"Tu" COMMAND—When an order is given to someone you address in the familiar form, i.e., someone to whom you say **tu**.

The affirmative imperative form is based on the present indicative: **-are** verbs have the same form as the 3rd person singular and **-ere** and **-ire** verbs have the same form as the 2nd person singular. The negative imperative form is the same as the verb's infinitive.

Affirmative	Negative
Parla!	Non parlare!
Speak!	*Don't speak!*
Scrivi!	Non scrivere!
Write!	*Don't write!*
Parti!	Non partire!
Leave!	*Don't leave!*

"Voi" COMMAND—When an order is given to two or more persons you address in the familiar form, i.e., to whom you would say **tu** individually.

The affirmative and the negative imperatives have the same form as the 2nd person plural of the present indicative.

Affirmative	Negative
Parlate!	Non parlate!
Speak!	*Don't speak!*
Scrivete!	Non scrivete!
Write!	*Don't write!*
Partite!	Non partite!
Leave!	*Don't leave!*

"Lei" COMMAND—When an order is given to a person you address in the formal form, i.e., to whom you say **Lei**.

The affirmative and negative imperatives have the same form as the 3rd person singular of the present subjunctive (see **What is the Subjunctive?**, p. 97).

Affirmative	Negative
Parli!	Non parli!
Speak!	*Don't speak!*

Scriva! Non scriva!
Write! *Don't write!*

Parta! Non parta!
Leave! *Don't leave!*

"LORO" COMMAND—When an order is given to two or more persons you address in the formal form, i.e., to whom you would say **Lei** individually.

The affirmative and negative imperatives have the same form as the 3rd person plural of the present subjunctive.

Affirmative	Negative
Parlino!	Non parlino!
Speak!	*Don't speak!*
Scrivano!	Non scrivano!
Write!	*Don't write!*
Partano!	Non partano!
Leave!	*Don't leave!*

"We" Command

This form is used to give commands or advice to oneself plus others.

The affirmative and negative imperatives have the same form as the 1st person plural of the present indicative.

Affirmative	Negative
Parliamo!	Non parliamo!
Let's speak!	*Let's not speak!*
Scriviamo!	Non scriviamo!
Let's write!	*Let's not write!*
Partiamo!	Non partiamo!
Let's leave!	*Let's not leave!*

Notice that the English phrase *let's* is not translated in Italian; the verb ending is the equivalent of *let's*.

Summary

For reference, here is a chart showing the affirmative and negative Italian command forms. Note that all of the imperative forms, except the **tu** forms, are the same in the affirmative and negative.

COMMAND FORM	AFFIRMATIVE	NEGATIVE
tu	present indicative -are → 3rd pers. sing. parla -ere, -ire → 2nd pers. sing. scrivi; parti	infinitive non parlare non scrivere; non partire
voi	present indicative 2nd pers. pl. parlate	 non parlate
Lei	present subjunctive 3rd pers. sing. parli	 non parli
Loro	present subjunctive 3rd pers. pl. parlino	 non parlino
noi	present indicative 1st pers. pl. parliamo	 non parliamo

▼▼▼▼▼▼▼▼▼▼▼▼▼▼▼▼▼▼▼▼REVIEW▼▼▼▼▼▼▼▼▼▼▼▼▼▼▼▼▼▼▼▼

I. Change the following sentences to an affirmative command.

1. You should study every evening.

_____

2. We go to the movies once a week.

_____

II. Change the following sentences to a negative command.

1. You shouldn't sleep in class.

_____

2. We don't talk in class.

_____

28. WHAT IS THE SUBJUNCTIVE?

The **subjunctive** is a mood used to express a wish, hope, uncertainty, or other similar attitude toward a fact or an idea. Since it stresses the speaker's feelings about the fact or idea, it expresses a "subjective" point of view.

IN ENGLISH

The subjunctive is only used in a very few constructions. Moreover, it is usually difficult to distinguish the forms of the subjunctive from other forms of the verb conjugation.

> I *am* in Detroit right now.
> present indicative of *to be*
> I wish I *were* in Rome right now.
> subjunctive same as past tense of *to be*

> He *reads* a book each week.
> present indicative of *to read*
> The professor insists that he *read* a book each week.
> subjunctive same as dictionary form of *to read*

The subjunctive occurs most commonly in the subordinate clause (see p. 101) of three kinds of sentences.

1. The subjunctive is used to express conditions contrary-to-fact, in clauses introduced by *if*.

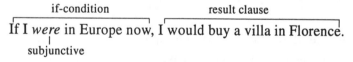

>   if-condition   result clause
> If I *were* in Europe now, I would buy a villa in Florence.
> subjunctive

2. The subjunctive is used in statements expressing a wish that is not possible.

> I wish he *were* here with us.
> subjunctive

3. The subjunctive, in this case the same as the dictionary form of the verb, is used following verbs of asking, demanding, and requesting.

> I asked that Maria *be* present.
> subjunctive

IN ITALIAN

The subjunctive, called the **congiuntivo**, is used very frequently in Italian. It has four tenses (**presente, passato, imperfetto, trapassato**) whose forms you must learn.

In only a few cases does the use of the **congiuntivo** correspond to the use of the subjunctive in English.

1. in conditions contrary-to-fact introduced by **se** *(if)*

> Se **fossi** ricco, comprerei una villa a Firenze.
> *If I were rich, I would buy a villa in Florence.*

2. following expressions of wish using **magari** *(if only)*

> Magari **fosse** qui con noi!
> *I wish he were here with us!*

3. following verbs of command (asking, urging, demanding, etc.)

> Esigo che Maria **sia** presente.
> *I demand that Maria be present.*

In Italian, the subjunctive is usually found in a dependent (subordinate) clause introduced by a main clause (p. 101) containing a specific type of verb or expression, or by a specific conjunction.

The following are the most frequent uses of the **congiuntivo**. (Note that in all of the examples below, the English equivalent of the **congiuntivo** is varied and never subjunctive.)

1. verbs of emotion, wish, command, opinion, doubt + **che** + subjunctive

> **Temo** che Marco non **arrivi** in tempo.
> verb of emotion   present subjunctive
> present indicative
>
> *I am afraid that Marco will not arrive on time.*
>   future

> Teresa **vuole** che il marito **cucini**.
>   verb of wish   present subjunctive
>   present indicative
>
> *Teresa wants her husband to cook.*
>   infinitive

Pensiamo che mamma **abbia** ragione.

verb of opinion   present subjunctive
present indicative

We think that Mother is right.

      present indicative

Dubito che **vinciate** la partita.

verb of doubt present subjunctive
present indicative

I doubt that you will win the game.

      future

2. impersonal verbs or expressions + **che** + subjunctive

Sembra che i miei amici **partano** presto per l'Europa.

impersonal verb   present subjunctive
present indicative

It seems that my friends are leaving soon for Europe.

      present progressive indicative

È possibile che papà **compri** una macchina nuova.

impersonal expression present subjunctive
present indicative

It is possible that Dad will buy a new car.

      future

3. certain conjunctions such as **perchè** *(so that)* , **benchè** *(although)*, **a condizione che** *(provided that)*, etc. + subjunctive

Apriamo la finestra **perchè entri** l'aria fresca.

present indicative conjunction present subjunctive

We are opening the window so (that) fresh air comes in.

      present indicative

Ti do il libro **a condizione che** tu me lo **restituisca** presto.

present indicative conjunction   present subjunctive

I will give you the book provided (that) you return it to me soon.

      present indicative

Study your textbook carefully for other uses of the subjunctive and its various tenses.

▼▼▼▼▼▼▼▼▼▼▼▼▼▼▼▼▼REVIEW▼▼▼▼▼▼▼▼▼▼▼▼▼▼▼▼▼

Indicate the appropriate mood in Italian for the verbs in italics: the indicative (I) mood or subjunctive (S) mood.

1. John wants Mary *to go out* with him. I S

2. I'm happy that you *have* a good job. I S

3. My mother says that Tom *is* a good student. I S

4. The doctor suggests that you *take* two aspirins for your fever. I S

5. It's important for you *to learn* Italian. I S

6. We doubt that he *won* the lottery. I S

7. I know that John *lives* in that house. I S

8. If I *were* you, I would go to class. I S

9. I'm sure that he *is* right. I S

10. It is strange that he *was* not at home. I S

29. WHAT IS THE CONDITIONAL?

The **conditional** is not found in English grammar books as a separate mood, but there is a mood in Italian called **condizionale** (see **What is Meant by Mood?**, p. 57). There are verb forms in English, however, which function the same as the "condizionale" in Italian and which can help you understand it. For practical purposes, we can call these forms the "present conditional" and the "past conditional."

Present Conditional

IN ENGLISH

The "present conditional" is a compound tense. It is formed with the auxiliary *would* + the dictionary form of the main verb: *I would like, they would close, we would buy.*

The "present conditional" is used in the following ways:

- to express polite wishes, requests, and preferences

> I *would like* to eat.
> *Would* you please lend me your book?
> I *would prefer* not to talk about it.

- in the **main clause** of a contrary-to-fact hypothetical statement in the present

> If I were rich, I *would buy* a Ferrari.

"I would buy a Ferrari" is a **clause** because it is composed of a group of words containing a subject *(I)* and a verb *(would buy)* and is used as part of a sentence. It is called the **main clause** because it expresses a complete thought and can stand by itself without being attached to the first part of the sentence ("If I were rich"). It is also called the **result clause** because it expresses what would happen as the result of being rich.

"If I were rich" is called the **subordinate clause**, or **if-clause**. It is a clause because it contains a subject *(I)* and a verb *(were)*; it is subordinate because it does not express a complete thought. Since it cannot stand alone, it is always found with a main clause.

The entire statement is called **hypothetical** because it refers to a condition that does not exist at the present time (the person speaking is not rich), but there is a remote possibility of its becoming a reality (the person speaking could be rich one day).

- in an indirect statement to express a **future-in-the-past**

  An **indirect statement** repeats, or reports, but does not quote, someone's words, as opposed to a **direct statement** which is a word-for-word quotation of what someone said. In written form a direct statement is always between quotation marks.

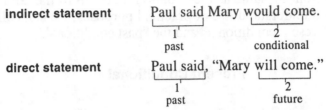

  In the indirect statement, action 2 is called a **future-in-the-past** because it takes place after another action in the past, action 1. In the direct statement, action 2 is merely a quotation of what was said.

Careful
The auxiliary *would* does not correspond to the conditional when it stands for *used to,* as in "She *would talk* while he painted." In this sentence, it means *used to talk* and requires the imperfect (see p. 80).

IN ITALIAN
You do not need an auxiliary to form the present conditional, called **condizionale**; it is a simple tense. It is formed with the future stem (see p. 86) + conditional endings: **chiederebbero** *(they would ask)*, **compreremmo** *(we would buy)*.

As in English, the "condizionale" is used in the following ways:

- to express polite wishes, requests, and preferences

  Vorrei mangiare.
  present conditional
  I would like to eat.

  Mi **presteresti** il tuo libro, per piacere?
  present conditional
  Would you please lend me your book?

  Preferirei non parlarne.
  present conditional
  I would prefer not to talk about it.

- in the main clause of a contrary-to-fact hypothetical statement in the present

> Se fossi ricco, *comprerei* una Ferrari.
> present conditional
> *If I were rich, I **would buy** a Ferrari.*

Past Conditional

IN ENGLISH

The "past conditional" is formed with the auxiliary *would have* + the past participle of the main verb *(I would have liked, they would have closed, we would have bought).*

The "past conditional" is used only in the main clause of a contrary-to-fact hypothetical statement in the past.

> If I had been rich, I *would have bought* a Ferrari.
> Contrary-to-fact: I did not buy a Ferrari because I was not rich.

Unlike some hypothetical statements in the present conditional where there is a possibility of their becoming a reality, all statements using the past conditional are **contrary-to-fact**; that is, the condition proposed was not fulfilled and the result is now seen as impossible.

IN ITALIAN

The past conditional, called **condizionale passato**, is formed with the auxiliary **avere** *(to have)* or **essere** *(to be)* in the present conditional + the past participle of the main verb: **mi sarebbe piaciuto** *(I would have liked),* **avrebbero chiuso** *(they would have closed),* **avremmo comprato** *(we would have bought).*

The past conditional is used:

- in the main clause of a contrary-to-fact hypothetical statement in the past

> Se fossi stato ricco, **avrei comprato** una Ferrari.
> past conditional
> *If I had been rich, I **would have bought** a Ferrari.*
> past conditional

As in English, all statements using the past conditional are contrary-to-fact in the past.

- in an indirect statement to express a future-in-the-past

> Paolo ha detto che Maria **sarebbe venuta**.
> past conditional
>
> *Paul said that Mary **would come**.*
> present conditional

Careful
Whereas English uses the "present conditional" to express a future-in-the-past, Italian uses the past conditional.

Sequence of Tenses in Hypothetical Statements

Let us study some examples of constructions with conditions and their results so that you learn to recognize them and to use the appropriate tense in Italian.

Hypothetical and contrary-to-fact statements are easy to recognize because they are made up of two clauses:

- the **if-clause**; that is, the subordinate clause introduced by *if* (**se** in Italian)

- the **result clause**; that is, the main clause (see p. 101)

The sequence of tenses is sometimes the same in both Italian and English. If you have difficulty recognizing tenses, just apply these three rules.

1. a hypothetical statement which expresses a possibility

IF-CLAUSE		RESULT CLAUSE	
present tense	+	future tense	ENGLISH
present tense	+	present tense	} ITALIAN
future tense	+	future tense	

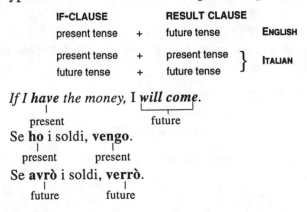

*If I **have** the money,* I **will come**.
present   future

Se **ho** i soldi, **vengo**.
present   present

Se **avrò** i soldi, **verrò**.
future   future

2. a hypothetical statement which is contrary-to-fact

- in the present (fulfillment of the condition is possible)

IF-CLAUSE		RESULT CLAUSE	
simple past	+	present conditional	ENGLISH
imperfect subjunctive	+	present conditional	ITALIAN

*If I **had** the money, I **would come**.*
⌐ ⌐
past   present conditional

Se **avessi** i soldi, **verrei**.
⌐ ⌐
imperfect   present conditional
subjunctive

- in the past (fulfillment of the condition is impossible)

IF-CLAUSE		RESULT CLAUSE	
past perfect	+	past conditional	ENGLISH
past perfect subjunctive	+	past conditional	ITALIAN

*If I **had had** the money, I **would have come**.*
⌐ ⌐
past perfect   past conditional

Se **avessi avuto** i soldi, **sarei venuto**.
⌐ ⌐
past perfect subjunctive   past conditional

Summary

Here is a reference chart of the sequence of tenses.

	ENGLISH	ITALIAN
	"if" clause + result clause	"if" clause + result clause
POSSIBLE	present + future	present + present or future + future
contrary-to-fact present → POSSIBLE	simple past + present conditional	imperfect + present subjunctive conditional
contrary-to-fact past → IMPOSSIBLE	past perfect + past conditional	past perfect + past subjunctive conditional

▼▼▼▼▼▼▼▼▼▼▼▼▼▼▼▼▼▼REVIEW▼▼▼▼▼▼▼▼▼▼▼▼▼▼▼▼▼▼

For each of the verbs in italics, identify the tense you would use in Italian: present (P), future (F), imperfect (I), present conditional (C), past conditional (PC), imperfect subjunctive (IS), past perfect subjunctive (PPS).

1. We (1) *would go* to Capri if we (2) *had* the money.

(1)	P	F	I	C	PC	IS	PPS
(2)	P	F	I	C	PC	IS	PPS

2. If they (1) *had studied*, they (2) *would have received* better grades.

(1)	P	F	I	C	PC	IS	PPS
(2)	P	F	I	C	PC	IS	PPS

3. When they were separated, he *would call* her every evening.

P	F	I	C	PC	IS	PPS

4. We (1) *will go* abroad, if we (2) *have* the money.

(1)	P	F	I	C	PC	IS	PPS
(2)	P	F	I	C	PC	IS	PPS

5. Tom promised that he *would do* it.

P	F	I	C	PC	IS	PPS

6. I know the children *would enjoy* that movie.

P	F	I	C	PC	IS	PPS

7. I *would like* some more meat, please.

P	F	I	C	PC	IS	PPS

8. If it (1) *rains,* they (2) *won't have* the picnic.

(1)	P	F	I	C	PC	IS	PPS
(2)	P	F	I	C	PC	IS	PPS

9. My parents wrote that they *would arrive* on July 10th.

P	F	I	C	PC	IS	PPS

30. WHAT IS A REFLEXIVE VERB?

A **reflexive verb** is a verb conjugated with a special pronoun called a **reflexive pronoun** which serves to "reflect" the action of the verb on the performer or subject. The result is that the subject, the verb, and the reflexive pronoun are in the same person.

He sees *himself* in the mirror.
We see *ourselves* in the mirror.

IN ENGLISH

Many verbs can take on a reflexive meaning by adding a reflexive pronoun.

Peter *cut* the paper.
regular verb

Peter *cut himself* when he shaved.
verb + reflexive pronoun

Pronouns ending with *-self* or *-selves* are used to make verbs reflexive. Here are the reflexive pronouns.

	Subject pronoun	Reflexive pronoun
Singular		
1st person	I	myself
2nd person	you	yourself
3rd person	he	himself
	she	herself
	it	itself
Plural		
1st person	we	ourselves
2nd person	you	yourselves
3rd person	they	themselves

In a sentence, the subject and the reflexive pronoun refer to the same "person."

I cut *myself.*
1st person singular

The rabbit tore *itself* free.
3rd person singular

Paul and Mary blamed *themselves* for the accident.

            3rd person plural

Although the subject pronoun *you* is the same in the singular and plural, the reflexive pronouns are different: *yourself* is used when you are speaking to one person (singular) and *yourselves* is used when you are speaking to more than one (plural).

Paul, did *you* hurt *yourself?*

          2nd person singular

Children, did *you* hurt *yourselves?*

          2nd person plural

IN ITALIAN

As in English, many regular verbs can be turned into reflexive verbs by adding a reflexive pronoun. Reflexive verbs have an infinitive form which has the reflexive pronoun **si** attached to it: **lavarsi** *(to wash oneself)*, **mettersi** *(to put on)*, **sentirsi** *(to feel)*.

Roberto **lava** la macchina.
*Robert **washes** the car.*

Roberto **si lava**.
*Robert **washes himself**.*

The dictionary lists **lavare** as the infinitive of *to wash* and **lavarsi** as the infinitive of *to wash oneself*.

Here are the reflexive pronouns in Italian.

mi	*myself*
ti	*yourself* [fam. sing.]
si	*himself, herself, yourself* [form. sing.]
ci	*ourselves*
vi	*yourselves* [fam. pl.]
si	*themselves, yourselves* [form. pl.]

Since the reflexive pronoun reflects the action of the verb back to the performer, the reflexive pronoun will change as the subject of the verb changes. You will have to memorize the conjugation of the reflexive verbs with the reflexive pronoun. Notice that, unlike English, where the reflexive pronoun is placed after the verb, in Italian the reflexive pronoun is usually placed immediately before the verb.

For example, the verb **lavarsi** is conjugated in the present indicative as follows:

Singular	Subject pronoun	Reflexive pronoun	Verb form
1st person	io	mi	lavo
2nd person	tu	ti	lavi
3rd person [form. sing.]	lui lei Lei	si	lava
Plural			
1st person	noi	ci	laviamo
2nd person	voi	vi	lavate
3rd person [form. pl.]	loro Loro	si	lavano

Reflexive verbs can be conjugated in all tenses. The subject pronoun and reflexive pronoun remain the same regardless of the verb tense; only the verb form changes: **lui si laverà** *(he will wash himself)*, **lui si è lavato** *(he washed himself)*.

The perfect tenses of reflexive verbs are always conjugated with the auxiliary **essere** *(to be)* and the past participle agrees in gender and number with the subject.

I bambini **si sono lavati**.
The children washed.

Maria **si è vestita** in fretta.
Mary got dressed in a hurry.

Use of Reflexive Verbs

Reflexive verbs are more common in Italian than in English; that is, there are many verbs that take a reflexive pronoun in Italian but not in English. For example, when you say in English, "Robert shaved" it is understood, but not stated, that "Robert shaved himself." In Italian the "himself" has to be stated. The English verb *to get up* also has a reflexive meaning: "Mary got up" means that she got herself up. In Italian you express *to get up* by using the verb **alzarsi,** that is **alzare** *(to raise)* + the reflexive pronoun **si** *(oneself)*.

There are many expressions which are not reflexive in English, but which require the use of a reflexive verb in Italian: *to have a good time* (**divertirsi**)*, to get dressed* (**vestirsi**)*, to sit down* (**sedersi**), etc.

▼▼▼▼▼▼▼▼▼▼▼▼▼▼▼▼REVIEW▼▼▼▼▼▼▼▼▼▼▼▼▼▼▼▼

I. Fill in the proper reflexive pronoun.

1. The children wash _____ every evening.

2. Carlo always blames _____.

3. Carlo, you always blame _____.

4. Children, behave _____.

5. We do everything to suit _____.

II. Refer to the chart on p. 109 and supply the appropriate reflexive pronoun in Italian.

1. Lei, Signora, _____ alza presto ogni mattina?

2. Io e Carlo _____ divertiamo molto assieme.

3. Tu _____ chiami Maria, vero?

4. Io _____ sono sentita male ieri sera.

5. Voi, ragazzi, _____ vestite sempre in fretta.

31. WHAT IS MEANT BY ACTIVE AND PASSIVE VOICE?

The **voice** of the verb refers to a basic relationship between the verb and its subject. There are two voices: active and passive.

THE ACTIVE VOICE—A sentence is said to be in the active voice when the subject is the performer of the action of the verb. In this instance, the verb is called an **active verb**.

> The teacher writes the exam.
>   subject   verb   direct object

> Paul ate an apple.
> subject verb direct object

> Lightning has struck the tree.
>   subject   verb   direct object

In all these examples, the subject performs the action of the verb and the direct object is the receiver of the action.

THE PASSIVE VOICE—A sentence is said to be in the passive voice when the subject is the receiver of the action. In this instance, the verb is called a **passive verb**.

> The exam is written by the teacher.
>   subject   verb   agent

> The apple was eaten by Paul.
>   subject   verb   agent

> The tree was struck by lightning.
>   subject   verb   agent

In all these examples, the subject is having the action of the verb performed upon it. The performer of the action, if it is mentioned, is introduced by the word *by*. The performer is called the **agent.**

IN ENGLISH

The passive voice is expressed by the verb *to be* conjugated in the appropriate tense + the past participle of the main verb (see p. 73). The tense of the passive sentence is indicated by the tense of the verb *to be.*

The exam *is written* by the teacher.

present

The exam *was written* by the teacher.

past

The exam *will be written* by the teacher.

future

IN ITALIAN

As in English, the passive voice can be expressed by the auxiliary verb **essere** (*to be*) conjugated in the appropriate tense + the past participle of the main verb. The tense of the passive sentence is indicated by the tense of the verb **essere**. The agent is introduced by **da.**

L'esame **è** preparato dal professore.

present

The exam is written by the teacher.

L'esame **è stato** preparato dal professore.

passato prossimo

The exam was written by the teacher.

L'esame **sarà** preparato dal professore.

future

The exam will be written by the teacher.

Because the auxiliary in the passive voice is always **essere**, all past participles in a passive sentence agree in gender and number with the subject.

I **vini** italiani sono **apprezzati** da tutti.

masc. pl.   masc. pl.

Italian wines are appreciated by everyone.

Changing an Active Sentence to a Passive Sentence

The steps to change an active sentence to a passive sentence are the same in English and in Italian.

1. The direct object of the active sentence becomes the subject of the passive sentence.

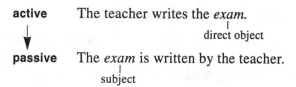

active   The teacher writes the *exam.*
                                    |
                               direct object

passive   The *exam* is written by the teacher.
                 |
              subject

2. The tense of the verb of the active sentence is reflected in the tense of the verb *to be* in the passive sentence.

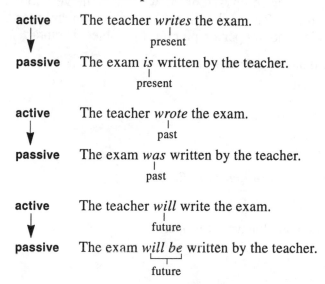

active   The teacher *writes* the exam.
                          |
                       present

passive   The exam *is* written by the teacher.
                     |
                  present

active   The teacher *wrote* the exam.
                          |
                        past

passive   The exam *was* written by the teacher.
                     |
                   past

active   The teacher *will* write the exam.
                         |
                      future

passive   The exam *will be* written by the teacher.
                     |___|
                      |
                    future

3. The subject of the active sentence becomes the agent of the passive sentence introduced with *by.*

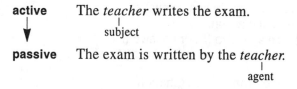

active   The *teacher* writes the exam.
                   |
                subject

passive   The exam is written by the *teacher.*
                                       |
                                     agent

Italian follows the same steps to change a sentence from active voice to passive voice.

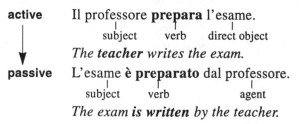

active   Il professore **prepara** l'esame.
              | | |
           subject   verb   direct object
           The teacher writes the exam.

passive   L'esame **è preparato** dal professore.
              | | |
           subject   verb   agent
           *The exam is **written** by the teacher.*

Avoiding the Passive Voice

Although the Italian language has a passive voice, it is not used as often as it is in English. Whenever possible, and particularly when the agent does not need to be emphasized, Italian tends to avoid the passive construction by using the active voice, or by using the **si**-construction.

The **si**-construction is composed of the word **si** + the verb in the 3rd person + the subject. The verb will in the 3rd person singular if the subject is singular, and 3rd person plural if the subject is plural.

*Italian **is spoken** in Switzerland.*
   subject   verb
   sing.   sing.

Si parla italiano in Svizzera.
    verb   subject
    sing.   sing.

*Many languages **are spoken** in Europe.*
    subject   verb
    pl.   pl.

Si parlano molte lingue in Europa.
    verb   subject
    pl.   pl.

▼▼▼▼▼▼▼▼▼▼▼▼▼▼▼▼▼REVIEW▼▼▼▼▼▼▼▼▼▼▼▼▼▼▼▼▼

Underline the subject in the sentences below.
- Circle the performer of the action.
- Identify each sentence as active (A) or passive (P).
- Identify the tense of the verb: present (P), past (PS), future (F).

1. Michelangelo painted the Sistine Chapel.   A P   P PS F

2. The bill is usually paid by Bob's parents.   A P   P PS F

3. The money was transferred by the bank.   A P   P PS F

4. Everyone will be going away during August.   A P   P PS F

5. The spring break will be enjoyed by all.   A P   P PS F

32. WHAT IS AN ADJECTIVE?

An **adjective** is a word that describes a noun, and in some cases a pronoun. The adjective is said to modify the noun or pronoun.

IN ENGLISH

Adjectives are classified according to the way they modify a noun or pronoun.

DESCRIPTIVE ADJECTIVE—A descriptive adjective indicates a quality; it describes the characteristics of the noun or pronoun (see p. 116).

> She read an *interesting* book.
> He has *brown* eyes.

POSSESSIVE ADJECTIVE—A possessive adjective indicates ownership of or relationship to a noun (see p. 124).

> *His* book is lost.
> *Our* parents are away.

INTERROGATIVE ADJECTIVE—An interrogative adjective asks a question about someone or something (see p. 131).

> *Which* teachers did you speak to?
> *What* book is lost?

DEMONSTRATIVE ADJECTIVE—A demonstrative adjective points out someone or something (see p. 133).

> *This* teacher is excellent.
> We went to Naples *that* summer.

IN ITALIAN

Adjectives are classified in the same way as in English. The principal difference is that in English adjectives generally do not change their form, while Italian adjectives must agree in gender and number with the noun or pronoun they modify.

33. WHAT IS A DESCRIPTIVE ADJECTIVE?

A **descriptive adjective** is a word that indicates a quality of a noun or pronoun. As the name implies, it *describes* the noun or pronoun.

The dress is *pretty*. It is bright *red*.
noun described   pronoun described

IN ENGLISH
The descriptive adjective does not change form, regardless of the noun or pronoun it modifies.

Mary bought an *expensive* book.
singular noun described

Mary bought *expensive* books.
plural noun described

In the above examples, the adjective *expensive* has the same form although in one instance it modifies a singular noun and in the other a plural noun.

Descriptive adjectives are divided into two groups depending on how they are connected to the noun they modify.

An **attributive adjective** is connected directly to its noun and always precedes it.

My family lives in a *white* house.
attributive   noun described
adjective

Good children are praised.
attributive   noun described
adjective

A **predicate adjective** is connected to the noun, or pronoun, it modifies by a linking verb, usually a form of *to be*. (Other common linking verbs are: *to seem, to feel, to smell, to sound, to taste, to become*.) The noun or pronoun modified by a predicate adjective is always the subject.

My house is *white*.
noun   linking   predicate adjective
subject   verb

They are *good.*

pronoun linking predicate adjective
subject verb

IN ITALIAN

Descriptive adjectives are classified in the same way as in English. The most important difference is that the adjective must agree with the noun or pronoun it modifies; that is, it must correspond in gender and number. Thus, the form of an adjective depends on whether the noun or pronoun is masculine or feminine, singular or plural.

Adjectives ending in **-o** change the final **-o** of the masculine singular to **-a** to form the feminine singular. For the plural, the masculine ending changes to **-i** and the feminine to **-e**. (Adjectives ending in **-e** change only to reflect the plural **-e** → **-i**.)

*the **red** dress*	il vestito **rosso**
	masc. masc.
	sing. sing.
*the **red** car*	la macchina **rossa**
	fem. fem.
	sing. sing.
*the **red** dresses*	i vestiti **rossi**
	masc. masc.
	pl. pl.
*the **red** cars*	le macchine **rosse**
	fem. fem.
	pl. pl.

As you can see in the examples above, in English, the attributive adjective *red* is placed before the noun it modifies whereas **rosso** is placed after the noun in Italian. This is not always the case; some Italian adjectives come before the noun they modify, the commonly used attributive adjective **buono** *(good)*, for example.

I **buoni** bambini sono lodati.

adjective noun

Good children are praised.

Refer to your textbook to learn which Italian attributive adjectives follow the noun they modify and which precede it.

Predicate adjectives always follow the linking verb and agree with the subject.

> I bambini sono **buoni**.
>   subject   adjective
>   — masc. pl.—
>
> *The children are good.*

> Lei è **ricca**; lui è **povero**.
> pronoun adj. pronoun adj.
> subject   subject
>   fem. sing.   masc. sing.
>
> *She is rich; he is poor.*

Nouns Used as Adjectives

IN ENGLISH

You should be able to recognize nouns used as adjectives; that is, a noun used to modify another noun. When a noun is used to describe another noun, the structure is as follows: the describing noun (i.e., the noun used as an adjective) + the noun described.

> Leather is expensive.   *Leather* goods are expensive.
>   noun   noun noun described
>   used as
>   adjective

> The desk is black.   The *desk* lamp is black.
>   noun   noun noun described
>   used as
>   adjective

IN ITALIAN

When a noun is used as an adjective, that is, to describe another noun, it remains a noun with its own gender and number and the structure is as follows: the noun described + a preposition (normally **in, da,** or **di**) + the describing noun.

> *leather* goods   prodotti **in pelle**
> *desk* lamp   lampada **da tavolo**

As you can see in these examples, a noun used as an adjective does not agree with the noun described.

▼▼▼▼▼▼▼▼▼▼▼▼▼▼▼▼REVIEW▼▼▼▼▼▼▼▼▼▼▼▼▼▼▼▼

I. Circle the adjectives in the sentences below.
- Draw an arrow from the adjective you circled to the noun or pronoun described.

1. Soccer is very popular in Europe.

2. The young woman was reading a newspaper on the crowded train.

3. We were very tired after our long walk.

4. Bill looked handsome in his dark suit yesterday.

5. The whole story soon became clear.

II. Underline the nouns used as adjectives.

1. Robert just bought a leather jacket.

2. He gave me a gold watch.

3. I need a new tennis racquet.

4. Our daughter loves chocolate cake.

5. Do you like tomato juice?

34. WHAT IS MEANT BY COMPARISON OF ADJECTIVES?

We compare adjectives when two or more nouns have the same quality (height, size, color, or any other characteristic) and we want to indicate that one of these nouns has a greater, lesser, or equal degree of this quality.[1]

```
              comparison of adjectives
          ┌──────────────┴──────────────┐
    Paul is tall but Mary is taller.
          │                      │
      adjective              adjective
      modifies Paul          modifies Mary
```

In both English and Italian there are two types of comparison: the comparative and the superlative.

Comparative

The comparative is used to compare the quality of one noun to the quality of another noun. There are three degrees of comparison.

IN ENGLISH
GREATER DEGREE—The comparison of greater degree (more) is formed differently depending on the length of the adjective being compared.

- short adjective + *-er* + *than*

  Paul is *taller than* Mary.
  Susan is *older than* her sister.

- *more* + longer adjective + *than*

  Mary is *more intelligent than* John.
  My car is *more expensive than* your car.

LESSER DEGREE—The comparison of lesser degree (less) is formed as follows: *less* + adjective + *than*

  John is *less intelligent than* Mary.
  Your car is *less expensive than* my car.

EQUAL DEGREE—The comparison of equal degree (same) is formed as follows → *as* + adjective + *as*

  Paul is *as tall as* John.
  My car is *as expensive as* his car.

---

[1] In English and in Italian the structure for comparing adverbs (see **What is an Adverb?**, p. 136) is the same as the structure for comparing adjectives.

IN ITALIAN

GREATER DEGREE—The comparison of greater degree is formed as follows: **più** + adjective + **di.**

> Giovanni è **più alto di** Roberto.
> *John is **taller than** Robert.*

> La mia macchina è **più cara della** tua macchina.
> *My car is **more expensive than** your car.*

LESSER DEGREE—The comparison of lesser degree is formed as follows: **meno** + adjective + **di.**

> Roberto è **meno alto di** Giovanni.
> *Robert is **less tall than** John.*

> La tua macchina è **meno cara della** mia macchina.
> *Your car is **less expensive than** my car.*

EQUAL DEGREE—The comparison of equal degree is formed as follows: **(tanto)** + adjective + **quanto** or **(così)** + adjective + **come.**

> Giovanni è **(tanto) alto quanto** Roberto.
> Giovanni è **(così) alto come** Roberto.
> *John is **as tall as** Robert.*

> La mia macchina è **(tanto) cara quanto** la tua macchina.
> La mia macchina è **(così) cara come** la tua macchina.
> *My car is **as expensive as** your car.*

Superlative

Superlative implies the highest or lowest degree of a quality. If that quality is compared to anyone or anything, it is called a relative superlative; if that quality is not compared to anyone or anything, it is called an absolute superlative.

Relative superlative

The relative superlative is the highest or lowest degree of a quality as compared to more than one person or thing.

IN ENGLISH

HIGHEST DEGREE—The relative superlative of highest degree is formed differently depending on the length of the adjectives:

- *the* + short adjective + *-est*

> John is *the tallest* of three brothers.
> My car is *the cheapest* on the market.

▪ *the most* + long adjective

> Mary is *the most intelligent* in the class.
> My car is *the most expensive* in the race.

LOWEST DEGREE—The relative superlative of lowest degree is formed as follows: *the least* + adjective.

> Robert is *the least tall* of his three brothers.
> My car is *the least expensive* in the race.

IN ITALIAN
HIGHEST DEGREE—The relative superlative of highest degree is formed as follows: the definite article + **più** + adjective + **di**.

> Giovanni è **il più alto dei** tre fratelli.
> *John is **the tallest of** the three brothers.*

> Questo bambino è **il più intelligente della** classe.
> *This child is **the most intelligent in the** class.*

LOWEST DEGREE—The relative superlative of lowest degree is formed as follows: the definite article + **meno** + adjective + **di.**

> Roberto è **il meno alto dei** tre fratelli.
> *Robert is **the least tall of the** three brothers.*

> La mia macchina è **la meno cara della** corsa.
> *My car is **the least expensive in the** race.*

Absolute Superlative

The **absolute superlative** is the highest degree of a quality without comparison to any other person or thing.

IN ENGLISH
The absolute superlative is formed by placing an intensifying adverb such as *very, extremely* + adjective.

> Dennis is *very tall.*
> My car is *extremely expensive.*

IN ITALIAN
The absolute superlative is usually formed as follows: adjective + **-issimo** or with **molto** *(very)*, **estremamente** *(extremely)*, **assolutamente** *(absolutely)* + adjective

> Dennis è **altissimo**.
> *Dennis is **very tall.***

La mia macchina è **estremamente cara.**
*My car is **extremely expensive.***

Careful

In English and in Italian a few adjectives have irregular forms of comparison which you will have to memorize individually.

adjective	*This apple is **bad.***
	Questa mela è **cattiva.**
comparative	*This apple is **worse.***
	not *badder
	Questa mela è **più cattiva.**
	Questa mela è **peggiore.**
superlative	*This apple is **the worst.***
	not *the baddest
	Questa mela è **la più cattiva.**
	Questa mela è **la peggiore.**

▼▼▼▼▼▼▼▼▼▼▼▼▼▼▼▼REVIEW▼▼▼▼▼▼▼▼▼▼▼▼▼▼▼▼

Underline the comparative and superlative adjective structures in the sentences below.
- Draw an arrow from the adjective to the noun or pronoun it modifies.
- Indicate the various degrees of comparison: comparative of greater degree (C+); comparative of equal degree (C=); comparative of lesser degree (C-); relative superlative of greatest degree (RS+), relative superlative of least degree (RS-); absolute superlative (AS).

1. Italy is extremely rich in art treasures.

    C+   C=   C-   RS+   RS-   AS

2. He is less intelligent than I am.

    C+   C=   C-   RS+   RS-   AS

3. Mary is as tall as Paul.

    C+   C=   C-   RS+   RS-   AS

4. That boy is the best in the school.

    C+   C=   C-   RS+   RS-   AS

35. WHAT IS A POSSESSIVE ADJECTIVE?

A **possessive adjective** is a word that indicates ownership of the noun it modifies. The owner is called the "possessor" and the noun modified is called the person or thing "possessed."

> Whose house is that? It's *my* house.
> possessor noun
> possessed

IN ENGLISH
Here are the forms of the possessive adjectives:

Singular

1st person		my
2nd person		your
3rd person	masc.	his
	fem.	her
	neuter	its

Plural

1st person	our
2nd person	your
3rd person	their

Possessive adjectives refer to the possessor.

> What color is John's car? *His* car is white.
> possessor singular

> What color is the Smiths' car? *Their* car is white.
> possessor plural

> Although the object possessed is the same *(car)*,
> the possessive adjective varies to agree with the possessor:
> John → singular, the Smiths → plural.

Possessive adjectives never change their form, regardless of the thing possessed.

> Mary is reading *my* magazine.
> object possessed singular

> Mary is reading *my* magazines.
> object possessed plural

Although the objects possessed are different in number
(magazine → singular; magazines → plural),
the possessive adjective is the same *(my).*

IN ITALIAN

As in English, an Italian possessive adjective refers to the possessor,
but unlike English, it must agree, like all Italian adjectives, in gender
and number with the noun it modifies, that is, the person or object
possessed. Also, Italian normally uses the definite article before the
possessive adjective. Therefore, the gender and number of the person
or object possessed is reflected in the definite article and the possessive adjective.

Maria is reading my magazine.
Maria sta leggendo **la** mia rivis**ta**.

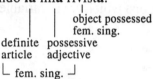

The possessive adjective **mia** is feminine singular
to agree with the feminine singular noun **rivista**.

Maria is reading my magazines.
Maria sta leggendo **le** mie rivis**te**.

		object possessed
		fem. pl.
definite	possessive	
article	adjective	

└ fem. pl. ┘

The possessive adjective **mie** is feminine plural
to agree with the feminine plural noun **riviste**.

These are the steps you should follow in order to choose the correct
possessive adjective and its proper form:

1. GENDER & NUMBER OF NOUN POSSESSED—Identify the gender and
   number of the person(s) or item(s) possessed.

2. POSSESSOR—Identify the possessor. Except for **loro** and **Loro** the
   possessor is shown by the first few letters of the possessive adjective.

my	**mi-**
your [fam. sing.]	**tu-**
his, her, its	**su-**
your [form. sing.]	**Su-**
our	**nostr-**
your [fam. pl.]	**vostr-**
their	**loro**
your [form. pl.]	**Loro**

3. DEFINITE ARTICLE—Depending on the gender and number of the noun possessed, place the appropriate definite article before the possessive adjective (see p. 15).

4. ENDING—Depending on the gender and number of the noun possessed, add the appropriate ending to the possessive adjective (except for **loro** and **Loro** which are invariable).

Singular

masculine	→	**-o**
feminine	→	**-a**

Plural

masculine	→	**-i** (except for **mi-** which adds **-ei**, and except for **tu-**, **su-**, and **Su-** which add **-oi**)
feminine	→	**-e**

5. SELECTION—The definite article + the possessive adjective + the noun possessed should agree in gender and number.

Below are examples of how these steps are applied to sentences with each possible possessor.

"MY"

> *I have my books.*
> 1. GENDER AND NUMBER OF NOUN POSSESSED:
>   **Libri** *(books)* is masculine plural.
> 2. POSSESSOR: my   **mi-**
> 3. & 4. DEFINITE ARTICLE & ENDING: **i + -ei**
> 5. SELECTION: **i miei libri**

Ho **i miei** libri.

"YOUR"—In the case of the possessive adjective *your*, you will have to consider additional factors:

> a. FAMILIAR OR FORMAL—Is the familiar or formal form of address appropriate (see p. 39)?

b. NUMBER—Does *your* address one person (singular) or more than one person (plural)?

Is this your house? [You are addressing a child.]
> 1. GENDER AND NUMBER OF NOUN POSSESSED:
>   **Casa** *(house)* is feminine singular.
> 2. POSSESSOR: your
>   a. FORMAL OR FAMILIAR: familiar   **tu-**
>   b. SINGULAR OR PLURAL: singular
> 3. & 4. DEFINITE ARTICLE & ENDING: **la + -a**
> 5. SELECTION: **la tua casa**

È questa **la tua** casa?

Is this your house? [You are addressing more than one child.]
> 1. GENDER AND NUMBER OF NOUN POSSESSED:
>   **Casa** *(house)* is feminine singular.
> 2. POSSESSOR: your
>   a. FORMAL OR FAMILIAR: familiar   **vostr-**
>   b. SINGULAR OR PLURAL: plural
> 3. & 4. DEFINITE ARTICLE & ENDING: **la + -a**
> 5. SELECTION: **la vostra casa**

È questa **la vostra** casa?

Is this your house? [You are addressing an adult.]
> 1. GENDER AND NUMBER OF NOUN POSSESSED:
>   **Casa** *(house)* is feminine singular.
> 2. POSSESSOR: your
>   a. FORMAL OR FAMILIAR: formal   **Su-**
>   b. SINGULAR OR PLURAL: singular
> 3. & 4. DEFINITE ARTICLE & ENDING: **la + -a**
> 5. SELECTION: **la Sua casa**

È questa **la Sua** casa?

Is this your house? [You are addressing more than one adult.]
> 1. GENDER AND NUMBER OF NOUN POSSESSED:
>   **Casa** *(house)* is feminine singular.
> 2. POSSESSOR: your
>   a. FORMAL OR FAMILIAR: formal   **Loro**
>   b. SINGULAR OR PLURAL: plural
> 3. DEFINITE ARTICLE: **la**
> 4. SELECTION: **la Loro casa**

È questa **la Loro** casa?

Since **Loro** is invariable, the gender and number of the possessive adjective are indicated only by the definite article.

"HIS, HER, ITS"—Since Italian possessive adjectives agree only with the noun possessed and therefore do not identify gender of the possessor, you will have to rely on context to determine whether *his, her,* or *its* is meant.

*Mary reads **her** books.*

1. GENDER AND NUMBER OF NOUN POSSESSED:
   Libri *(books)* is masculine plural.
2. POSSESSOR: her   **su-**
3.&4. DEFINITE ARTICLE & ENDING: **i + -oi**
5. SELECTION: **i suoi libri**

Maria legge **i suoi** libri.

*Mario reads **his** books.*

1. GENDER AND NUMBER OF POSSESSED:
   Libri *(books)* is masculine plural.
2. POSSESSOR: his   **su-**
3.& 4. DEFINITE ARTICLE & ENDING: **i + -oi**
5. SELECTION: **i suoi libri**

Mario legge **i suoi** libri.

The possessive adjective agrees with the items possessed (**libri**); so that *her books* and *his books* will be **i suoi libri**. Only the context, in this case the names *Maria* and *Mario,* reveals the gender of the possessor.

"OUR"

Our house is downtown.

1. GENDER AND NUMBER OF NOUN POSSESSED:
   Casa *(house)* is feminine singular.
2. POSSESSOR: our   **nostr-**
3. & 4. DEFINITE ARTICLE & ENDING: **la + -a**
5. SELECTION: **la nostra casa**

La nostra casa è in centro.

"THEIR"—Since **loro** is invariable, the gender and number of the possessive adjective are indicated only by the definite article.

This is their house.

1. GENDER AND NUMBER OF NOUN POSSESSED:
   Casa *(house)* is feminine singular.
2. POSSESSOR: their   **loro**
3. DEFINITE ARTICLE: **la**
4. SELECTION: **la loro casa**

Questa è **la loro** casa.

*These are **their** houses.*

1. GENDER AND NUMBER OF NOUN POSSESSED:
   Case *(houses)* is feminine plural.
2. POSSESSOR: their **loro**
3. DEFINITE ARTICLE: **le**
4. SELECTION: **le loro case**

Queste sono **le loro** case.

Summary

Here is a chart of the possessive adjectives you can use as reference.

Possessor	SINGULAR		PLURAL	
	masculine	feminine	masculine	feminine
my	il mio	la mia	i miei	le mie
your [fam. sing.]	il tuo	la tua	i tuoi	le tue
his, her, its	il suo	la sua	i suoi	le sue
your [form. sing.]	il Suo	la Sua	i Suoi	le Sue
our	il nostro	la nostra	i nostri	le nostre
your [fam. pl.]	il vostro	la vostra	i vostri	le vostre
their	il loro	la loro	i loro	le loro
your [form.pl.]	il Loro	la Loro	i Loro	le Loro

▼▼▼▼▼▼▼▼▼▼▼▼▼▼▼▼▼REVIEW▼▼▼▼▼▼▼▼▼▼▼▼▼▼▼▼▼

Circle the possessive adjectives in the sentences below.
- Draw an arrow from the possessive adjective to the noun it modifies.
- Circle the number of the possessive adjective: singular (S) or plural (P).
- Fill in the possessive adjective in the Italian sentences below.

1. Teresa lost my notebook.

NOUN MODIFIED IN ITALIAN: masculine   S   P

Teresa ha perso _____ quaderno.

2. Our teacher is from Rome.

NOUN MODIFIED IN ITALIAN: feminine   S   P

_____ professoressa è di Roma.

3. Andrew, where are your gloves?

NOUN MODIFIED IN ITALIAN: masculine   S   P

Andrea, dove sono _____ guanti?

4. Their house is very comfortable.

NOUN MODIFIED IN ITALIAN: feminine   S   P

_____ casa è comoda.

5. He sold his bicycles.

NOUN MODIFIED IN ITALIAN: feminine   S   P

Ha venduto _____ biciclette.

36. WHAT IS AN INTERROGATIVE ADJECTIVE?

An **interrogative adjective** is a word that asks a question about a noun.

Which teacher do you have?
|
noun

IN ENGLISH

The words *which, what* and *how much, how many* are interrogative adjectives when they precede a noun and are used to ask a question about that noun. (When they are not followed by a noun they are interrogative pronouns, see p. 163.)

> *What* courses are you taking?
> *Which* newspaper do you prefer to read?
> *How much* coffee do you drink?
> *How many* children were there?

IN ITALIAN

There are three interrogative adjectives: 1. **che** corresponding to the English *what;* 2. a form of **quale** corresponding to *which;* 3. a form of **quanto** corresponding to *how much, how many.*

1. to ask a general question: *what* (or *which*) + noun → **che** + noun

   Che is invariable; it does not agree in gender and number with the noun it modifies.

   > **Che** giornale leggi?
   > *What newspaper do you read?*

   > **Che** corsi frequenti?
   > *What courses are you taking?*

2. to ask a question implying a choice between two or more alternatives: *which* (or *what*) + noun → a form of **quale** + noun

   Quale agrees only in number with the noun it modifies; it does not agree in gender.

   > **Quale** giornale preferisci leggere?
   >   singular
   > **Which** newspaper do you prefer to read? [among these three]

   > **Quali** dischi porti?
   >   plural
   > **Which** records are you bringing? [among this pile]

3. to ask *how much* or *how many* + noun → a form of **quanto** + noun

Quanto (-a, -i, -e) has four forms to agree in gender and number with the noun it modifies.

Quanto caffè bevi?
masculine singular
How much coffee do you drink?

Quante valigie porti?
feminine plural
How many suitcases are you taking?

▼▼▼▼▼▼▼▼▼▼▼▼▼▼▼▼▼▼REVIEW▼▼▼▼▼▼▼▼▼▼▼▼▼▼▼▼▼▼

Circle the interrogative adjectives in the sentences below.
■ Draw an arrow from the interrogative adjective to the noun it modifies.
■ Circle the number of the interrogative adjective: singular (S) or plural (P).
■ Fill in the interrogative adjective in the Italian sentences below.

1. How much time do you have?

NOUN MODIFIED IN ITALIAN: masculine   S   P

_____ tempo hai?

2. Which car are we taking, yours or mine?

NOUN MODIFIED IN ITALIAN: feminine   S   P

_____ macchina prendiamo, la tua o la mia?

3. What brand of coffee do you usually buy?

NOUN MODIFIED IN ITALIAN: feminine   S   P

_____ marca di caffè compri di solito?

4. How many brothers does she have?

NOUN MODIFIED IN ITALIAN: masculine   S   P

_____ fratelli ha?

37. WHAT IS A DEMONSTRATIVE ADJECTIVE?

A **demonstrative adjective** is a word used to point out a person or an object.

> *This* book is more interesting than *that* book.

IN ENGLISH

The demonstrative adjectives are *this* or *these* which point out a person or an object near the speaker and *that* or *those* which point out a person or an object away from the speaker. They are a rare example of adjectives agreeing in number with the noun they modify: *this* which is used before a singular noun changes to *these* before a plural noun and *that* changes to *those*.

> *this* cat   →   *these* cats
> *that* man   →   *those* men

IN ITALIAN

As in English, there are two sets of demonstrative adjectives: one set for persons or objects close to the speaker, and one for those far from the speaker. However, each set has four forms which agree in gender and number with the nouns they modify.

1. noun near the speaker: *this, these* → a form of **questo**

> *Do you see **this** boy?*
>> To say "*this* boy" in Italian, begin by analyzing the Italian equivalent for the noun modified **ragazzo** *(boy)*. Since **ragazzo** is masculine singular, the demonstrative adjective will be masculine singular → **questo**.

> Vedi **questo** ragazzo?
>>   masc.   masc.
>>   sing.   sing.

> *Do you see **these** houses?*
>> To say "*these* houses" in Italian begin by analyzing the Italian equivalent for the noun modified **case** *(houses)*. Since **case** is feminine plural, the demonstrative adjective will be feminine plural → **queste**

> Vedi **queste** case?
>>   fem.   fem.
>>   pl.   pl.

Here is a chart of the four basic forms you can use as a reference.

Singular		
masculine	questo	*this*
feminine	questa	
Plural		
masculine	questi	*these*
feminine	queste	

2. noun away from the speaker → a form of **quello**

In addition to the four basic forms, a different demonstrative adjective is used depending on the letter, or letters, with which the noun begins. (They follow the same pattern as the definite article, p. 15.)

To choose the correct demonstrative adjective begin by studying the noun modified.

    1. Gender and number of the noun modified?
    2. Beginning letter(s) of noun modified—There are 3 possibilities:
        —before "z" or "s" + consonant
        —before any other consonant
        —before a vowel

Here are some examples:

    *Do you see **that** student?*
        1. GENDER & NUMBER: **Studente** *(student)* is masculine singular.
        2. BEGINNING LETTER(S)—**Studente** begins with "s" + consonant.
    Vedi **quello** studente?

    *Do you see **those** trees?*
        1. GENDER & NUMBER: **Alberi** *(trees)* is masculine plural.
        2. BEGINNING LETTER(S)—**Alberi** begins with a vowel.
    Vedi **quegli** alberi?

Here is a chart you can use as reference.

	Before "z" or "s" + consonant	Before any other consonant	Before a vowel	
Singular				
masculine	quello	quel	quell'	*that*
feminine	quella	quella	quell'	
Plural				
masculine	quegli	quei	quegli	*those*
feminine	quelle	quelle	quelle	

▼▼▼▼▼▼▼▼▼▼▼▼▼▼▼REVIEW▼▼▼▼▼▼▼▼▼▼▼▼▼▼▼▼▼

Circle the demonstrative adjectives in the sentences below.
- Draw an arrow from the demonstrative adjective to the noun it modifies.
- Circle the number of the noun modified: singular (S) or plural (P).
- Write the initial letter of the noun modified, where required.
- Fill in the demonstrative adjective in the Italian sentences below.

1. Where did you buy that watch?

NOUN MODIFIED IN ITALIAN: masculine   S   P

INITIAL LETTER OF NOUN MODIFIED: _____

Dove hai comprato _____ orologio?

2. I like this magazine.

NOUN MODIFIED IN ITALIAN: feminine   S   P

Mi piace _____ rivista.

3. They play soccer in that stadium.

NOUN MODIFIED IN ITALIAN: masculine   S   P

INITIAL LETTER OF NOUN MODIFIED: _____

Giocano a calcio in _____ stadio.

4. Lucia gave me these records.

NOUN MODIFIED IN ITALIAN: masculine   S   P

Lucia mi ha regalato _____ dischi.

5. I remember those years well.

NOUN MODIFIED IN ITALIAN: masculine   S   P

INITIAL LETTER OF NOUN MODIFIED: _____

Ricordo molto bene _____ anni!

38. WHAT IS AN ADVERB?

An **adverb** is a word that describes a verb, an adjective, or another adverb.[1]

Mary drives *well*.
    verb   adverb

The house is *very* big.
    adverb adjective

The girl ran *too quickly*.
    adverb adverb

IN ENGLISH

There are different types of adverbs:

- adverbs of manner answer the question *how*? They are the most common adverbs and can usually be recognized by their **-ly** ending.

     Mary sings *beautifully*.
     Beautifully describes the verb *sings*, how Mary sings.

     They parked the car *carefully*.
     Carefully describes the verb *parked*, how the car was parked.

- adverbs of quantity or degree answer the question *how much?*

     Paul is *quite* studious.

- adverbs of time answer the question *when?*

     He will be home *soon*.

- adverbs of place answer the question *where?*

     I left my books *there*.

IN ITALIAN

Adverbs must be memorized as vocabulary. The adverbs of manner can be recognized by their ending **-mente** which corresponds to the English ending *-ly*.

natural**mente**	*naturally*
general**mente**	*generally*
rapida**mente**	*rapidly*

---

[1] In English and in Italian the structure for comparing adverbs is the same as the structure for comparing adjectives (see **What is Meant by Comparison of Adjectives?**, p. 120).

The most important fact for you to remember is that adverbs are invariable; this means that they never become plural, nor do they have gender.

Adverb or Adjective?

You can identify a word as an adverb or adjective by looking at the word modified:

- if it modifies a verb, an adjective, or an adverb → adverb
- if it modifies a noun or a pronoun → adjective

> *The **beautiful** diva sang **beautifully**.*
>
> > *Beautiful* modifies the noun *diva*; it is an adjective. *Beautifully* modifies the verb *sang*; it describes how she sang; it is an adverb.

It is particularly important to distinguish adverbs from adjectives in Italian since adverbs are invariable, but adjectives must agree with the noun they modify.

> *Maria speaks **a lot**.*
> modifies *speak*, a verb → adverb
> Maria parla **molto**.
> adverb (invariable)

> *Maria speaks **very** well.*
> modifies *well*, an adverb → adverb
> Maria parla **molto** bene.
> adverb (invariable)

> *Maria is **very** conscientious.*
> modifies *conscientious,* an adjective → adverb
> Maria è **molto** diligente.
> adverb (invariable)

But:

> *Maria speaks **many** languages.*
> modifies *languages,* a noun → adjective
> Maria parla **molte** lingue.
> adjective   noun
> fem. pl.   fem. pl.

Careful

In colloquial English adjectives are often used instead of adverbs. For instance, we hear "they spoke *loud*" instead of *loudly;* "he drove *slow*" instead of *slowly.* In Italian you don't have a choice, you must use the adverb in these cases.

Remember that in English *good* is an adjective; *well* is an adverb.

> The boy writes *good* English.
>> *Good* modifies the noun *English* → adjective

> The student writes *well.*
>> *Well* modifies the verb *writes* → adverb

Likewise, in Italian **buono** is an adjective meaning *good;* **bene** is the adverb meaning *well.*

> *It's a **good** car and it runs **well**.*
>   adjective   adverb

> È una **buona** macchina e va **bene.**
>   adjective   adverb
>   fem. sing.

▼▼▼▼▼▼▼▼▼▼▼▼▼▼▼▼▼▼REVIEW▼▼▼▼▼▼▼▼▼▼▼▼▼▼▼▼▼▼

Circle the adverbs in the sentences below.

- Draw an arrow from the adverb to the word it modifies.

1. The students arrived early.

2. Paul learned the lesson very quickly.

3. The students were too tired to study.

4. He has a reasonably secure income.

5. Mary is a good student who speaks Italian quite well.

39. WHAT IS A PREPOSITION?

A **preposition** is a word that shows the relationship of one word (usually a verb, a noun or pronoun) to another word in the sentence. The noun or pronoun following the preposition is called the **object of the preposition**. The preposition plus its object is called a **prepositional phrase**.

prepositional phrase

The teacher was *in* the classroom.

object of the preposition

IN ENGLISH

Prepositions normally indicate position, direction, or time.

- prepositions showing position

> Paul was *in* the car.
> Mary put the books *on* the table.

- prepositions showing direction

> Mary went *to* school.
> The students came directly *from* class.

- prepositions showing time

> Italian people go on vacation *in* August.
> *Before* class, they went to eat.

Not all prepositions are single words:

because of	in front of	instead of
due to	in spite of	on account of

The meaning of a preposition is often determined by its context. Notice the different meanings of the preposition "on" in the following sentences: she lives *on* the floor above, John was *on* time, he spoke *on* writing.

In all the sentences above, the preposition comes before its object. However, the position of a preposition in an English sentence may vary and the preposition may be placed after its object. Spoken English often places a preposition at the end of the sentence; in this position it is called a **dangling preposition**. In formal English we usually try to avoid a dangling preposition by placing it within the sentence before its object or at the beginning of a question.

Spoken English	$\rightarrow$	Formal English

The man I spoke *to* is Italian.   The man *to whom* I spoke is Italian.

Who are you going *with?*   *With whom* are you going?

Here is the book you asked *about.*   Here is the book *about which* you asked.

IN ITALIAN

You will have to memorize prepositions as vocabulary. As in English, prepositions have a different meaning depending on their context.

There are three important things to remember:

1. Prepositions are invariable. They never become plural, nor do they have a gender.

2. Prepositions are tricky. Every language uses prepositions differently. Do not assume that the same preposition is used in Italian as in English, or even that a preposition is used in Italian when one is used in English (and vice versa).

ENGLISH	$\rightarrow$	ITALIAN

change of prepositions

to laugh *at*   ridersi **di** *(of)*

to be married *to*   essere sposato **con** *(with)*

same   **different**

preposition   **prepositions**

to go *to* Florence   andare **a** Firenze

to go *to* Italy   andare **in** Italia

to go *to* Luciano's   andare **da** Luciano

preposition   **no preposition**

to look *for*   cercare

to look *at*   guardare

to pay *for*   pagare

no preposition   **preposition**

to approach   avvicinarsi **a**

to enter   entrare **in**

An Italian dictionary will give you the verb plus the preposition when one is required. In the case of an English verb followed by a preposition, be careful not to translate it into Italian word-for-word. For example, to find the word for *to look for*, do not stop at the first dictionary entry for *look* which is **guardare** and then add the preposition *per* corresponding to *for.* Continue searching for the specific form *look for* which corresponds to the verb **cercare,** used without a preposition.

I am looking for Frank
Cerco Franco

On the other hand, when looking up verbs such as *enter, telephone, trust,* be sure to include the Italian preposition which you will you find listed in the dictionary entry.

Mary is entering the classroom.
Maria entra **in** classe.

3. Although in an English sentence the position of a preposition may vary, in Italian, the position of a preposition is set: a preposition is always placed within a sentence before its object. There are no dangling prepostions. With regard to prepositions, Italian has the same structure as formal English.

The man I speak to is my uncle.
To man to whom I speak is my uncle.
L'uomo **a** cui parlo è mio zio.

Who are you playing with?
With whom are you playing?
Con chi giochi?

▼▼▼▼▼▼▼▼▼▼▼▼▼▼▼▼REVIEW▼▼▼▼▼▼▼▼▼▼▼▼▼▼▼▼▼

I. Circle the prepositions in the following sentences.

1. The students didn't understand what the lesson was about.

2. The professor had come from Sicily by boat.

3. The teacher walked around the room as she talked.

4. Contrary to popular opinion, he was a good student.

5. The garden between the two houses was very small.

II. Write the restructured sentence that parallels the structure of the Italian sentence.

1. Richard is the boy I was talking about.

_____

2. I got the scholarship I applied for.

_____

40. WHAT IS A CONJUNCTION?

A **conjunction** is a word that links words or groups of words.

IN ENGLISH
There are two kinds of conjunctions: coordinating and subordinating.

Coordinating conjunctions join words, phrases, and clauses that are equal; they coordinate elements of equal rank. The major coordinating conjunctions are *and, but, or, nor, for,* and *yet.*

> good *or* evil
> over the river *and* through the woods
> They invited us, *but* we couldn't go.

Subordinating conjunctions join a dependent clause to a main clause; they subordinate one clause to another (see p. 101). A clause introduced by a subordinating conjunction is called a **subordinate clause.** Typical subordinating conjunctions are *before, after, since, although, because, if, unless, so that, while, that,* and *when.*

> *Although* we were invited, we didn't go.
> subordinating   main
> conjunction   clause

> They left *because* they were bored.
> main   subordinating
> clause   conjunction

> He said *that* he was tired.
> main   subordinating
> clause conjunction

Notice that the subordinate clause may come before or after the main clause.

IN ITALIAN
Conjunctions must be memorized as vocabulary items. Like adverbs and prepositions, conjunctions are invariable; that is, they never change their form.

Subordinating Conjunction or Preposition?

In English, the same word may sometimes function as either a subordinating conjunction or a preposition; in Italian, however, a different word would normally be required for each function.

We can distinguish between a subordinating conjunction and a preposition simply by determining if the word introduces a prepositional phrase (see p. 139) or a subordinate clause.

For instance, *before* can be used as a subordinating conjunction and as a preposition in English. In Italian, however, as a subordinating conjunction *before* is **prima che**, but **prima** as a preposition.

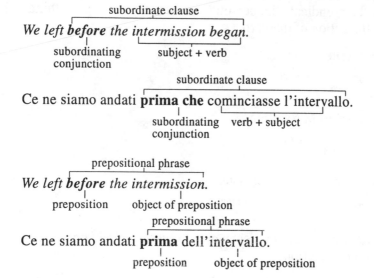

▼▼▼▼▼▼▼▼▼▼▼▼▼▼▼▼▼REVIEW▼▼▼▼▼▼▼▼▼▼▼▼▼▼▼▼▼

Circle the coordinating and subordinating conjunctions in the sentences below.
- Underline the words each conjunction serves to coordinate or to subordinate.

1. Mary and Paul were going to study French or Italian.

2. She did not study because she was too tired.

3. After the concert is over, we will go home.

4. They borrowed money so they could go to Rome.

5. After the concert, unless you are too tired, we'll go for a drink.

41. WHAT ARE OBJECTS?

Every sentence consists, at the very least, of a subject and a verb. This is called the **sentence base**.

John writes.
She spoke.

The subject of the sentence is usually a noun or pronoun. Many sentences contain other nouns or pronouns that are related to the action of the verb or to a preposition. These nouns or pronouns are called **objects**. They indicate the person (or persons), or thing (or things) that receive the action of the verb.

Paul writes a letter.
subject | verb | object

Paul writes Mary often.
subject | verb | object

Paul goes out with her sister.
subject | verb | object

There are three types of objects: direct object, indirect object, and object of a preposition.

Direct Object

IN ENGLISH

A **direct object** is a noun or pronoun that receives the action of the verb directly, without a preposition between the verb and the following noun or pronoun. It answers the question *what?* or *whom?* asked after the verb.[1]

Paul writes *a letter*.
QUESTION: Paul writes what? ANSWER: A letter.
A letter is the direct object.

They see *Paul and Mary*.
QUESTION: They see whom? ANSWER: Paul and Mary.
Paul and Mary are the two direct objects.

---

[1]In this section, we will consider active sentences only. (See **What is Meant by Active and Passive Voice?**, p.111.)

Do not assume that any word that comes right after a verb is the direct object. For it to be the direct object it must answer the question *what?* or *whom?*

John writes well.

QUESTION: John writes what? ANSWER: No answer.
QUESTION: John writes whom? ANSWER: No answer.

There is no direct object in the sentence.
Well is an adverb; it answers the question: John writes *how?*

Verbs can be classified as to whether or not they take a direct object.

▪ a **transitive verb** is a verb that takes a direct object

The boy *threw* the ball.
　　　　 |　　　　 |
　　transitive verb　direct object

▪ an **intransitive verb** is a verb that does not take a direct object

Paul *is sleeping.*
　　|_____|
　　intransitive verb

IN ITALIAN

As in English, a direct object is a noun or pronoun that receives the action of the verb directly, without a preposition. It answers the question **che (cosa)?** *(what?)* or **chi?** *(whom?)* asked after the verb.

Giovanni scrive **una lettera**.
John writes a letter.

Vedono **Paolo e Maria**.
They see Paul and Mary.

Indirect Object

IN ENGLISH

An **indirect object** is a noun or pronoun that receives the action of the verb indirectly, through the preposition "to" or "for." It answers the two-word question *to* or *for whom?* or *to* or *for what?* asked after the verb.

John writes *to his brother.*

QUESTION: John writes to whom? ANSWER: To his brother.
His brother is the indirect object.

Sometimes the word *to* is not included in the English sentence.

John writes *his brother*.

IN ITALIAN
As in English, an indirect object is a noun or pronoun that receives the action of the verb indirectly. It answers the two-word question *to whom?* or *to what?* asked after the verb. Nouns that are indirect objects are easy to identify in Italian because they are always preceded by the preposition **a**.

Giovanni scrive **a suo fratello**.
John writes his brother.

Sentences With a Direct and Indirect Object

A sentence may contain both a direct object and an indirect object.

IN ENGLISH
When a sentence has both a direct and indirect object, the following two word orders are possible:

1. subject (s) + verb (v) + indirect object (io) + direct object (do)

Paul gave his sister a gift.
   s   v   io   do

QUESTION: Who gave a gift? ANSWER: Paul.
Paul is the subject.

QUESTION: Paul gave what? ANSWER: A gift.
A gift is the direct object.

QUESTION: Paul gave a gift to whom? ANSWER: His sister.
His sister is the indirect object.

2. subject + verb + direct object + *to* + indirect object

Paul gave a gift to his sister.
   s   v   do *to*   io

The first structure is the most common. However, because there is no "to" preceding the indirect object, it is more difficult to identify its function than in the second structure. Be sure to ask the questions to establish the function of objects in a sentence.

IN ITALIAN

When a sentence contains both a direct and an indirect object noun, the word order is usually subject + verb + direct object + **a** + indirect object.

Giovanni scrive **una lettera a suo fratello**.
| | | | | |
S   V   DO   **a**   IO

*John writes **his brother a letter**.*
*John writes **a letter to his brother**.*

Notice that the direct object noun precedes the indirect object noun.

Object of a Preposition

IN ENGLISH

An **object of a preposition** is a noun or pronoun that follows a preposition other than "to." (Objects of the preposition "to" are called indirect objects.) It answers the question *what?* or *whom?* asked after the preposition.

John went *with Mary*.

> QUESTION: John went with whom? ANSWER: With Mary.
> *Mary* is the object of the preposition *with*.

They entered the house through *the window*.

> QUESTION: They entered through what? ANSWER: Through the window.
> *The window* is the object of the preposition *through*.

IN ITALIAN

As in English, an object of a preposition is a noun or pronoun that receives the action of the verb through a preposition other than **a** *(to)*.

Giovanni è andato **con Maria**.
*John went **with Mary**.*

Sono entrati in casa **dalla finestra**.
*They entered the house **through the window**.*

Careful

The relationship between verb and object is often different in English and Italian. For example, a verb may take an object of a preposition in English, but a direct object in Italian. It is important that you pay close attention to such differences when you learn Italian verbs. Your textbook, as well as dictionaries, will indicate when an Italian verb is followed by a preposition.

Here are some examples.

- **Object of a preposition in English → Direct object in Italian**

    *I am looking **for the book**.*
    FUNCTION IN ENGLISH: object of a preposition
    QUESTION: I am looking for what? ANSWER: The book.
    The book is the object of the preposition *for*.

    Cerco **il libro**.
    FUNCTION IN ITALIAN: direct object
    QUESTION: Che cerco? ANSWER: Il libro.
    Since the verb **cercare** is not followed by a preposition,
    il libro *(the book)* is a direct object.

Many common verbs require an object of a preposition in English but a direct object in Italian.

*to look **at***	guardare
*to wait **for***	aspettare
*to pay **for***	pagare

- **Direct object in English → Indirect object in Italian**

    *She calls **her friends** every day.*
    FUNCTION IN ENGLISH: direct object
    QUESTION: She calls whom? ANSWER: Her friends.
    Her friends is the direct object of *calls*.

    Telefona **ai suoi amici** ogni giorno.
    FUNCTION IN ITALIAN: indirect object
    QUESTION: A chi telefona ogni giorno? ANSWER: Ai suoi amici.
    Since the verb is **telefonare a**,
    suoi amici *(her friends)* is an indirect object.

A few common verbs require a direct object in English but an indirect object in Italian.

to obey	obbedire **a**
to resemble	somigliare **a**
to approach	avvicinarsi **a**

- **Direct object in English → Object of a preposition in Italian**

    *Mary's parents remember **the war**.*
    FUNCTION IN ENGLISH: direct object
    QUESTION: Mary's parents remember what? ANSWER: The war.
    The war is the direct object.

    I genitori di Maria si ricordano **della guerra**.
    di + la

FUNCTION IN ITALIAN: object of preposition
QUESTION: Di che si ricordano i genitori di Maria?
ANSWER: Della guerra.
Since the verb is **ricordarsi di,**
la guerra *(the war)* is the object of the preposition **di.**

A few common verbs require a direct object in English but an object of a preposition in Italian.

to enter	entrare **in**
to trust	fidarsi **di**
to doubt	dubitare **di**

▪ Subject in English → Indirect object in Italian

With some Italian verbs (V), the equivalent of a subject (S) in English is an indirect object (IO) in Italian, and the equivalent of a direct object (DO) in English is a subject (S) in Italian. This is the case of the English verb *to like* (**piacere,** literally *to be pleasing*).

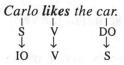

A Carlo **piace** la macchina.
to Carlo is pleasing the car

Let us go over this type of transformation step by step:

1. TRANSFORMATION—Transform the English sentence by turning the subject (S) into an indirect object (IO) and the direct object (DO) into the subject (S).

    Carlo likes the car. → The car is pleasing to Carlo.
      S   V   DO   S   V   IO

2. PLACEMENT—Place the indirect object at the beginning of the sentence.

    "to Carlo is pleasing the car"
      IO   V   S

You can now express that structure in Italian.

"to Carlo is pleasing the car"

A Carlo piace la macchina.
  IO   V   S

Here is a list of the common verbs which require an indirect object in Italian where English uses a subject.

to be sorry	dispiacere
to need	occorrere
to be lacking	mancare

Since Italian and English patterns do not coincide in many cases, it is important to identify the object function within the language in which you are working.

Summary

The different types of objects in a sentence can be identified by looking to see if they are introduced by a preposition and, if so, by which one.

DIRECT OBJECT—An object that receives the action of the verb directly, without a preposition.

INDIRECT OBJECT—An object that receives the action of the verb indirectly, through the preposition *to* or *for*.

OBJECT OF A PREPOSITION—An object that receives the action of the verb through a preposition other than *to* or *for.*

Your ability to recognize the three kinds of objects is essential. With pronouns, for instance, a different Italian pronoun is used for the English pronoun *him* depending on whether *him* is a direct object (**lo**), an indirect object (**gli**) or an object of a preposition (**lui**).

▼▼▼▼▼▼▼▼▼▼▼▼▼▼▼▼▼REVIEW▼▼▼▼▼▼▼▼▼▼▼▼▼▼▼▼▼

Next to Q, write the question you need to ask to find the object.
- Next to A, write the answer to the question you just asked.
- In the column to the right, identify the kind of object it is: direct object (DO), indirect object (IO), or object of a preposition (OP).

1. We will invite our friends.

   Q: _____

   A: _____ DO IO OP

2. The audience watched the opera with enthusiasm.

   Q: _____

   A: _____ DO IO OP

   Q: _____

   A: _____ DO IO OP

3. The father read his children a story.

   Q: _____

   A: _____ DO IO OP

   Q: _____

   A: _____ DO IO OP

4. Stefano left his friends a message at the desk.

   Q: _____

   A: _____ DO IO OP

   Q: _____

   A: _____ DO IO OP

   Q: _____

   A: _____ DO IO OP

42. WHAT IS AN OBJECT PRONOUN?

An **object pronoun** is a pronoun used as an object of a verb or of a preposition.

    Mary saw *me* at school.

IN ENGLISH

Pronouns change according to their function in the sentence. Pronouns used as subjects are studied in **What is a Subject Pronoun?**, p. 36. We use subject pronouns when we conjugate verbs (see **What is a Verb Conjugation?**, p. 42). Object pronouns are used when a pronoun is either a direct object, indirect object, or object of a preposition (see **What are Objects?**, p. 144).

Except for the pronoun "you," the form of the object pronoun is different from the form of the subject pronoun, but the same pronoun form is used as a direct object, indirect object, or object of a preposition.

	Subject Pronouns	Object Pronouns
singular		
1st person	I	me
2nd person	you	you
3rd person	he	him
	she	her
	it	it
plural		
1st person	we	us
2nd person	you	you
3rd person	they	them

Here are a few examples. As you can see, the object pronoun is always placed after the verb or after the preposition.

    She saw *me*.
        direct object → object pronoun

    I lent *him* my car.
        indirect object → object pronoun

    They went out with *her*.
        object of a preposition → object pronoun

IN ITALIAN

Unlike English a different object pronoun is normally used for each kind of object: direct, indirect, and object of a preposition. You will, therefore, have to establish the function of a pronoun so that you can choose the correct Italian form.

Italian Direct Object Pronouns

First, you have to establish that the Italian verb takes a direct object. Remember that English and Italian verbs don't always take the same type of objects and that when working in Italian you will have to establish the type of object taken by the Italian verb (see p. 148).

Let us look at the Italian direct object pronouns.

Direct Object Pronouns

Singular

Ist person		**mi**	*me*
2nd person		**ti**	*you* [familiar]
3rd person	masc.	**lo**	*him, it*
	fem.	**la**	*her, it*
	masc./fem.	**La**	*you* [formal]

Plural

Ist person		**ci**	*us*
2nd person		**vi**	*you* [familiar]
3rd person	masc.	**li**	*them*
	fem.	**le**	*them*
	masc.	**Li**	*you* [formal]
	fem.	**Le**	*you* [formal]

Direct object pronouns are used as they are in English, but normally they precede the conjugated verb. Consult your textbook for rules about placement.

To see how direct object pronouns are selected, we have divided them into two categories: the ones that are merely a question of memorization and those which require analysis.

"ME, HIM, HER, US"

These direct object pronouns are merely a question of memorization. Select the form you need and place it before the conjugated verb:
me → **mi**, him → **lo**, her → **la**, us → **ci.**

> *John sees me.*
> Giovanni **mi** vede.

*John sees **him**.*
Giovanni **lo** vede.

"You"—There are various equivalents of the object pronoun *you* depending on the person or persons being addressed. Follow these steps to select the proper form.

1. FORM—Is the familiar or formal form of "you" appropriate?

If familiar:

2. NUMBER—Are you addressing one or more persons?
   - one person → singular → **ti**
   - more than one person → plural → **vi**

If formal:

2. NUMBER—Are you addressing one or more persons?
   - one person → singular → **La**
   - if more than one person → plural: What is their gender?

3. GENDER—Are you addressing men or women?
   - a group of men or men and women → masculine → **Li**
   - a group of women → feminine → **Le**

Here are a few examples.

*Maria, John sees **you** often.* [You = Maria]
    1. *Maria* implies familiarity → familiar
    2. *Maria* is one person → singular
Maria, Giovanni **ti** vede spesso.

*Boys, John sees **you** often.* [You = boys]
    1. *Boys* implies familiarity → familiar
    2. *Boys* is more than one person → plural
Ragazzi, Giovanni **vi** vede spesso.

*Sir, John sees **you** often.* [You = Sir]
    1. *Sir* implies formality → formal
    2. *Sir* is one person → singular
Signore, Giovanni **La** vede spesso.

*Mrs. Rossi, John sees **you** often.* [You = Mrs. Rossi]
    1. *Mrs. Rossi* implies formality → formal
    2. *Mrs. Rossi* is one person → singular
Signora Rossi, Giovanni **La** vede spesso.

*Gentlemen, John sees **you** often.* [You = Gentlemen]
  1. *Gentlemen* implies formality → formal
  2. *Gentlemen* is more than one person → plural
  3. *Gentlemen* is masculine

Signori, Giovanni **Li** vede spesso.

*Young ladies, John sees **you** often.* [You = young ladies]
  1. *Young ladies* implies formality → formal
  2. *Young ladies* is more than one person → plural
  3. Feminine

Signorine, Giovanni **Le** vede spesso.

"IT"—The form will depend on the gender of its antecedent, i.e., the noun "it" refers to: masculine antecedent → **lo**; feminine antecedent → **la.**

*Do you see the plane? Yes, I see **it**.*
  1. ANTECEDENT: **L'aero** *(plane)*
  2. GENDER: masculine
  3. SELECTION: **lo**

Vedi l'aero? Si, **lo** vedo.

*Do you see the car? Yes, I see **it**.*
  1. ANTECEDENT: **la macchina** *(car)*
  2. GENDER: feminine
  3. SELECTION: **la**

Vedi la macchina? Si, **la** vedo.

"THEM"—The form will depend on the gender of its antecedent, i.e. the noun "them" refers to: masculine antecedent → **li**; feminine antecedent → **le.**

*Do you see the boys? Yes, I see **them**.*
  1. ANTECEDENT: **i ragazzi** *(boys)*
  2. GENDER: masculine
  3. SELECTION: **li**

Vedi i ragazzi? Si, **li** vedo.

*Do you see the cars? Yes, I see **them**.*
  1. ANTECEDENT: **le macchine** *(cars)*
  2. GENDER: feminine
  3. SELECTION: **le**

Vedi le macchine? Si, **le** vedo.

Italian Indirect Object Pronouns

First, you have to establish that the Italian verb takes an indirect object. Remember that English and Italian verbs don't always take the same type of objects and that when working in Italian you will have to establish the type of object taken by the Italian verb (see p. 148).

Let us look at the Italian indirect object pronouns.

Indirect Object Pronouns

Singular

Ist person		mi	*to me*
2nd person		ti	*to you* [familiar]
3rd person	masc.	gli	*to him*
	fem.	le	*to her*
	masc./fem.	Le	*to you* [formal]

Plural

Ist person	ci	*to us*
2nd person	vi	*to you* [familiar]
3rd person	loro	*to them*
	Loro	*to you* [formal]

To see how indirect object pronouns are selected, we have divided them into two categories: the ones that are merely a question of memorization and those which require analysis.

"ME, HIM, HER, US, THEM"

These indirect object pronouns are merely a question of memorization. Select the form you need and place it before the conjugated verb: to me → **mi**, to him → **gli**, to her → **le**, to us → **ci**, to them → **loro.**

When a pronoun is used, the "to" preceding the English indirect object is not expressed in Italian. The Italian indirect object pronoun means "to me," "to you," etc. Except for **loro** and **Loro** which are placed after the verb, the indirect object pronouns normally precede the conjugated verb. Consult your textbook for further rules.

Here are a few examples.

> *John gives the book to me.*
> *John gives me the book.*

1. IDENTIFY THE VERB: to give
2. SELECT THE ITALIAN EQUIVALENT: **dare**
3. IDENTIFY THE PRONOUN OBJECT: me

QUESTION: John gives the book to whom? ANSWER: To me.
Me is an indirect object pronoun.

4. SELECT THE ITALIAN EQUIVALENT: **mi**

Giovanni **mi** da il libro.

John gives the book to him.
John gives him the book.
Giovanni **gli** da il libro.

John gives the book to them.
John gives them the book.
Giovanni da **loro** il libro.
|
placed after the verb (**da**)

"You"—There are various equivalents of the object pronoun *you* depending on the person or persons being addressed. Follow these steps to select the proper form.

1. FORM—Is the familiar or formal form of "you" appropriate?

If familiar:

2. NUMBER—Are you addressing one or more persons?
- one person → singular → **ti**
- more than one person → plural → **vi**

If formal:

2. NUMBER—Are you addressing one or more persons?
- one person → singular → **Le**
- if more than one person → plural → **Loro**

Here are a few examples.

Ragazze,
John is giving the book to you. [You = girls]
John is giving you the book.
Giovanni **vi** da il libro.

Sir (Madam),
John is giving the book to you. [You = Sir or Madam]
John is giving you the book.
Signore (Signora),
Giovanni **Le** da il libro.

Gentlemen (Young ladies),
*John is giving the book **to you**.* [You = Gentlemen or Young ladies]
*John is giving **you** the book.*
Signori (Signorine)
Giovanni da **Loro** il libro.
      |
    placed after the verb (**da**)

Italian Object of Preposition Pronouns

First, you have to establish that the Italian verb is followed by a preposition. The object of preposition pronouns are used after a preposition other than the preposition *to* or *for.* Remember that English and Italian verbs don't always take the same type of objects and that when working in Italian you will have to establish the type of object taken by the Italian verb (see p. 148).

Let us look at the Italian object of preposition pronouns. (Note that, except for **me** and **te**, the forms are the same as the subject pronouns.)

Object of Preposition Pronouns

Singular			
lst person		prep. + me	*prep. + me*
2nd person		prep. + te	*prep. + you* [familiar]
3rd person	masc.	prep. + lui	*prep. + him*
	fem.	prep. + lei	*prep. + her*
		prep. + Lei	*prep. + you* [formal]

Plural		
lst person	prep. + noi	*prep. + us*
2nd person	prep. + voi	*prep. + you* [familiar]
3rd person	prep. + loro	*prep. + them*
	prep. + Loro	*prep. + you* [formal]

To see how pronoun objects of a preposition are selected, we have divided them into two categories: the ones that are merely a question of memorization and those which require analysis.

"ME, HIM, HER, US, THEM"
These object of preposition pronouns are merely a question of memorization. Select the form you need and place it after the verb preceded by the appropriate preposition : me → **me**, him → **lui**, her → **lei**, us → **noi**, them → **loro**.

Here are a few examples.

> *Are they talking about Luigi? No, they are talking **about me**.*
> 1. IDENTIFY THE PREPOSITION: about (**di**)
> 2. IDENTIFY THE OBJECT OF THE PREPOSITION: me
> 3. SELECTION: **me**

Parlano di Luigi? No, parlano **di me**.

> *Are you going to the party with Mary? Yes, I'm going **with her**.*
> Vai alla festa con Maria? Si, vado **con lei**.

> *Did you receive a letter from your friends?*
> *Yes, I received a letter **from them** yesterday.*
> Hai ricevuto una lettera dai tuoi aimici?
> Si, ho ricevuto una lettera **da loro** ieri.

"You"—There are various equivalents of the object of preposition pronoun *you* depending on the person or persons being addressed. Follow these steps to select the proper form.

1. FORM—Is the familiar or formal form of "you" appropriate?

If familiar:

2. NUMBER—Are you addressing one or more persons?
   - one person → singular → **te**
   - more than one person → plural → **voi**

If formal:

2. NUMBER—Are you addressing one or more persons?
   - one person → singular → **Lei**
   - if more than one person → plural → **Loro**

Here are some examples.

> *Carla, I would like to speak **with you**.*
> Carla, vorrei parlare **con te**.

> *Boys, I would like to speak **with you**.*
> Ragazzi, vorrei parlare **con voi**.

> *Miss, I would like to speak **with you**.*
> Signorina, vorrei parlare **con Lei**.

> *Gentlemen, I would like to speak **with you**.*
> Signori, vorrei parlare **con Loro**.

In Italian a noun referring to a thing is not generally replaced by a pronoun when it follows a preposition. For example, in answer to the question "Is the book on the table?" one does not say "Yes, the book is *on it*." Rather, one repeats the noun: "Yes, the book is *on the table*." Similarly, in answer to the question "Do you live near the mountains?" one does not usually say, "Yes, I live *near them*." Instead, one repeats the noun: "Yes, I live *near the mountains*."

Careful

Remember that English and Italian verbs don't always take the same type of objects and that when working in Italian you will have to establish the type of object taken by the Italian verb (see p. 148).

Stressed and Unstressed Pronouns

The direct and indirect object pronouns already treated in this chapter are called **conjunctive** or **unstressed pronouns** and they usually precede the verb.

The object of preposition forms of the pronoun are also used for emphasis or contrast in place of the direct or indirect object pronouns. In this function, they are called **disjunctive** or **stressed pronouns** and they are placed after the verb.

> *I see her.* [unstressed]
> **La** vedo.
> |
> unstressed pronoun
> direct object
> precedes the verb (**vedo**)

> *I see her.* [stressed: "I see her and no one else."]
> Vedo **lei**.
> |
>   stressed pronoun
>   direct object
>   follows the verb (**vedo**)

> *I gave the book to her.* [unstressed]
> **Le** ho dato il libro.
> |
> unstressed pronoun
> indirect object
> precedes the verb (**ho dato**)

I gave the book to her. [stressed: "I gave the book to her and to no one else."]
Ho dato il libro **a lei**.

             stressed pronoun
             indirect object
             follows the verb (**ho dato**)

Summary

Here is a chart of subject and object pronouns that you can use as reference :

		UNSTRESSED		STRESSED &
		DIRECT	INDIRECT	OBJECT OF
	SUBJECT	OBJECT	OBJECT	PREPOSITION
singular 1st person	io	mi	mi	me
2nd person	tu	ti	ti	te
(m.) 3rd pers. (f.)	lui lei Lei	lo la La	gli le Le	lui lei Lei
plural 1st person	noi	ci	ci	noi
2nd person	voi	vi	vi	voi
3rd pers.	loro Loro	li (m.) le (f.) Li (m.) Le (f.)	loro Loro	loro Loro

Object pronouns are difficult to handle. Consult your textbook for additional rules.

▼▼▼▼▼▼▼▼▼▼▼▼▼▼▼▼▼REVIEW▼▼▼▼▼▼▼▼▼▼▼▼▼▼▼▼▼

Underline the object pronoun.
- Using the chart on pp. 161, indicate the Italian equivalent: direct object (DO), indirect object (IO), or object of a preposition (OP); singular (S), or plural (P).
- Fill in all the blanks.

1. Luisa likes that song and she sings it often.

   to sing → **cantare**

FUNCTION OF PRONOUN IN ENGLISH:	DO	IO	OP
FUNCTION OF PRONOUN IN ITALIAN:	DO	IO	OP

   ANTECEDENT IN ENGLISH: _____

   GENDER OF ANTECEDENT IN ITALIAN: feminine

   NUMBER OF ANTECEDENT IN ITALIAN: S   P

   A Luisa piace quella canzone e _____ canta spesso.

2. Why don't you come with me?

   to come → **venire**

FUNCTION OF PRONOUN IN ENGLISH:	DO	IO	OP
FUNCTION OF PRONOUN IN ITALIAN:	DO	IO	OP

   Perchè non vieni con _____ ?

3. Did you write Paul? No, I will write him a letter today.

   to write → **scrivere**

FUNCTION OF PRONOUN IN ENGLISH:	DO	IO	OP
FUNCTION OF PRONOUN IN ITALIAN:	DO	IO	OP

   Hai scritto a Paolo? No, _____ scriverò una lettera oggi.

4. Have you called your parents? No, I will call them today.

   to call, telephone → **telefonare a**

FUNCTION OF PRONOUN IN ENGLISH:	DO	IO	OP
FUNCTION OF PRONOUN IN ITALIAN:	DO	IO	OP

   Hai telefonato ai tuoi genitori? No, telefonerò _____ domani.

43. WHAT IS AN INTERROGATIVE PRONOUN?

An **interrogative pronoun** is a word that replaces a noun and introduces a question.

> This is a nice house. *Who* lives here?

IN ENGLISH
Different interrogative pronouns are used depending on whether you are referring to a "person" (this category includes human beings and live animals) or a "thing" (this category includes objects and ideas). Also, the interrogative pronoun referring to persons changes according to its function in the sentence.

IN ITALIAN
As in English, a different interrogative pronoun is used depending on whether the pronoun replaces a person or a thing. Also, as in English, an interrogative pronoun can be a subject, a direct object, an indirect object, or an object of a preposition.

"Who, whom"

IN ENGLISH
Who is used for the subject of the sentence.

> *Who* lives here?
> |
> subject

Whom is used for the direct object, indirect object, and the object of a preposition.

> *Whom* do you know here?
> |
> direct object

> To *whom* did you speak?
> |
> indirect object

> From *whom* did you get the book?
> |
> object of preposition *from*

In colloquial English, *who* is often used instead of *whom*, and prepositions are placed at the end of the sentence, separated from the interrogative pronoun to which they are linked.

Who do you know here?
|
instead of *whom*

Who did you speak to?
| |
instead of *whom*   preposition

Who did you get the book from?
| |
instead of *whom*   preposition

IN ITALIAN

***Who* or *whom* → chi**

Chi vive qui?
Who lives here?

Chi conosci qui?
Whom do you know here?

When the interrogative pronoun is used as an indirect object it is preceded by the preposition **a**. It will therefore be necessary to restructure the sentence.

Who *are you speaking to?* → ***To whom*** *are you speaking?*
| |
subject form of   preposition   object form of interrogative
interrogative

A chi parli?

When the interrogative pronoun is used as an object of a preposition it is preceded by the preposition. It will therefore be necessary to restructure the sentence.

Who *did you get the book from?* → ***From whom*** *did you get the book?*

Da chi hai avuto il libro?

"Whose"

IN ENGLISH

Whose is the possessive form and is used to ask about possession or ownership.

Whose pencil is this?
|
possessive

They are nice cars. *Whose* are they?
|
possessive

IN ITALIAN

Whose → **di chi**. To use the correct word order in Italian, restructure the question by replacing *whose* with "of whom" and invert the word order of the subject and verb.

> *Whose car is it?*
> **Di chi** è la macchina?
> [word-for-word: *of whom is the car*]

> *Whose keys are they?*
> **Di chi** sono le chiavi?
> [word-for-word: *of whom are the keys*]

"What"

IN ENGLISH

What refers only to things, and the same form is used for subject, direct object, indirect object, and the object of a preposition.

> *What* happened?
> subject

> *What* do you want?
> direct object

> *What* do you cook with?
> object of preposition *with*

IN ITALIAN

What → **che** or **che cosa**, or just **cosa**. They are interchangeable and invariable. The same form is used for subject, direct object, indirect object, and the object of a preposition.

> *What happened?*
> **Che** è successo?

> *What do you want?*
> **Che** vuoi?

> *What do you cook with?*
> *With what do you cook?*
> **Con che** cucini?

"Which one, which ones"

IN ENGLISH

Which one, *which ones* can refer to both persons and things; they are used in questions that request the selection of one (*which one*, singular) or several (*which ones*, plural) from a group. The words *one* and *ones* are often omitted. These interrogative pronouns may be used as a subject, direct object, indirect object, and object of a preposition.

There are two teachers here. *Which one* teaches Italian?
singular subject

I have two cars. *Which one* do you want to take?
singular direct object

There are many children here. *Which ones* do you want to play *with?* →
Restructured: With *which ones* do you want to play?
plural object of the preposition *with*

IN ITALIAN

Which one, *which ones* → **quale, quali.** There are two forms to agree in number with the noun replaced, *which one* (singular) or *which ones* (plural). If the English word *one* or *ones* is not expressed, look at the verb to establish number: if the verb is singular → **quale**; if the verb is plural → **quali**.

> *There are two teachers are here. **Which one** teaches Italian?*
> Ci sono due insegnanti qui. **Quale** insegna italiano?

> *I have two cars. **Which one** do you want to take?*
> Ho due macchine. **Quale** vuoi prendere?

> *There are many children here. With **which ones** do you want to play?*
> Ci sono molti bambini qui. Con **quali** vuoi giocare?

"What is...? What are...?" "Che" vs. "Quale"

Questions beginning with "what is...?" or "what are" can be translated into Italian by either **che + essere...?** or **quale (quali) + essere...?** depending on what the expected answer will be.

- when the expected answer is a definition → **che + essere...?**

> *What is poetry?*
> The expected answer is a definition of poetry.
> **Che** è la poesia?

- when the expected answer is one of a number of choices and answers the question *which one(ones)* of many → **quale** (**quali**) + **essere...?**

    What is your favorite novel?

    The expected answer will explain which novel of the many that exist is your favorite.

    Quale è il tuo romanzo preferito?

There is another interrogative pronoun that we will now examine separately since it does not follow the same pattern as above.

"How much, how many"

IN ENGLISH

These interrogative pronouns are a rare example of pronouns that change form to agree in number with the noun they replace: *how much* (singular), *how many* (plural).

I have some money. *How much* do you need?
                    └────┬────┘
                    singular pronoun

I have some stamps. *How many* do you need?
                     └────┬────┘
                     plural pronoun

IN ITALIAN

This interrogative pronoun has four forms that change according to the gender and number of the antecedent, that is, the noun replaced by the pronoun: singular → **quanto** (**-a**); plural → **quanti** (**-e**).

Let us look at a few examples.

*I have some money today. **How much** do you want?*
  1. IDENTIFY ANTECEDENT: **denaro** *(money)*
  2. GENDER OF ANTECEDENT: masculine
  3. NUMBER OF ANTECEDENT: singular
  4. SELECTION: **quanto**

Ho del denaro oggi. **Quanto** vuoi?

*There were ten students present. **How many** voted in favor?*
  1. IDENTIFY ANTECEDENT: **studenti** *(students)*
  2. GENDER OF ANTECEDENT: masculine
  3. NUMBER OF ANTECEDENT: plural
  4. SELECTION: **quanti**

C'erano dieci studenti presenti. **Quanti** hanno votato a favore?

▼▼▼▼▼▼▼▼▼▼▼▼▼▼▼▼▼REVIEW▼▼▼▼▼▼▼▼▼▼▼▼▼▼▼▼▼

Underline the interrogative pronouns in the questions below.
- Restructure the English sentence.
- Indicate the function of the interrogative pronoun in the Italian sentence: subject (S), object (O), or possessive (P).
- Fill in the Italian equivalent of the interrogative.

1. What a nice car! Whose is it?

RESTRUCTURE THE SENTENCE: _____

FUNCTION: S   O   P

Che bella macchina! _____ è?

2. Who are you talking to?

RESTRUCTURE THE SENTENCE: _____

FUNCTION: S   O   P

Con _____ parli?

3. Who did you see last night?

RESTRUCTURE THE SENTENCE: _____

FUNCTION: S   O   P

_____ hai visto ieri sera?

44. WHAT IS A DEMONSTRATIVE PRONOUN?

A **demonstrative pronoun** is a word that replaces a noun previously mentioned, the **antecedent**, as if pointing to it. Demonstrative comes from *demonstrate,* to show.

> Which book are you buying? *This one.*
> antecedent

IN ENGLISH

English demonstrative pronouns change form according to the number of the noun they replace and according to the relationship of that noun with the speaker.

As with the demonstrative adjectives, ***this (one), these*** refer to persons or objects near the speaker; ***that (one), those*** to persons or objects away from the speaker.

> Here are two suitcases. *This one* is big and *that one* is small.
> The books are on the shelves. *These* are in Italian, *those* in English.

IN ITALIAN

Demonstrative pronouns are related to the demonstrative adjectives (see **What is a Demonstrative Adjective?**, p. 133): forms of **questo** or **quello**.

TO POINT OUT ↓	SINGULAR		PLURAL	
	masc.	**fem.**	**masc.**	**fem.**
items near the speaker *this (one), these*	questo	questa	questi	queste
items away from the speaker *that (one), those*	quello	quella	quelli	quelle

As pronouns, these words replace the demonstrative adjective + noun; they will agree in number and gender with the noun replaced.

To choose the correct form, follow these steps.

1. ANTECEDENT—Determine the antecedent.
2. GENDER & NUMBER—Determine the gender and number of the antecedent.
3. SELECTION—Based on Steps 1 and 2 choose the correct form from the chart.

Let us apply these steps to some examples.

> *Which book do you want? **This one.***
> 1. Antecedent: **libro** *(book)*
> 2. Gender & number: masculine singular
> 3. Selection: **questo**

Quale libro vuoi? **Questo**.

> *Which houses did you build? **These.***
> 1. Antecedent: **case** *(houses)*
> 2. Gender & number: feminine plural
> 3. Selection: **queste**

Quali case hai costruito? **Queste**.

> *Which book do you want? **That one.***
> 1. Antecedent: **libro** *(book)*
> 2. Gender & number: masculine singular
> 3. Selection: **quello**

Quale libro vuoi? **Quello**.

> *Which houses did you build? **Those.***
> 1. Antecedent: **case** *(houses)*
> 2. Gender & number: feminine plural
> 3. Selection: **quelle**

Quali case hai costruito? **Quelle**.

There is another demonstrative pronoun which we will now examine separately because it does not follow the same pattern as above.

"The One, the ones"

IN ENGLISH

The demonstrative pronouns *the one* and *the ones*, unlike *this one* and *that one*, do not point out a specific object, but instead introduce a clause (see p. 101) that gives us additional information about an object and helps us identify it. There is a singular form *the one* and a plural form *the ones*. They are often followed by the relative pronoun *that* or *which* (see **What is a Relative Pronoun?**, p. 175).

> Which house did you buy? *The one* over there.
> Clause: "the one over there" gives us additional information about the house.
> Number: *The one* is singular.

What books do you want? *The ones (that)* I gave you.
> CLAUSE: "the ones that I gave you" gives us additional information about
> the   book. Notice that the relative pronoun *that* can be omitted.
> NUMBER: *The ones* is plural.

IN ITALIAN

The equivalent of the English pronouns *the one, the ones* is a form of
the Italian demonstrative pronoun **quello.** It can be used in two ways:
1. to introduce a clause and 2. to show possession.

In both cases, follow these steps to choose the correct form of **quello.**

1. ANTECEDENT—Find the antecedent.

2. GENDER & NUMBER—Determine the gender and number of the
   antecedent.

3. SELECTION— Based on steps 1 and 2, choose the appropriate
   form.

1. to introduce a clause

> *Which house did you buy? **The one** over there.*
> > 1. ANTECEDENT: **casa** *(house)*
> > 2. GENDER & NUMBER: feminine singular
> > 3. SELECTION: **quella**
>
> Quale casa hai comprato? **Quella** là.

> *Which books do you want? **The ones** I gave you.*
> > 1. ANTECEDENT: **libri** *(books)*
> > 2. GENDER & NUMBER: masculine plural
> > 3. SELECTION: **quelli**
>
> Quali libro vuoi? **Quelli** che ti ho dato.

2. to show possession

> Because the possessive cannot be expressed in Italian with the Eng-
> lish apostrophe structure (see **What is the Possessive?**, p. 21), an
> alternative structure is used which is equivalent to "the one of."

> Just as "my father's house" can only be expressed in Italian by a
> structure which is word-for-word "the house of my father," the
> phrase "my father's" is expressed by a structure which is word-for-
> word "*the one of* my father." In this case also **quello** agrees in
> gender and number with its antecedent, here "the house."

Let us apply the rules to the following examples.

Which house are you selling? My father's.

My father's → *the one* of my father
1. ANTECEDENT: house (**casa**)
2. GENDER & NUMBER : **casa** is feminine singular.
3. SELECTION: **quella**

Quale casa vendi? **Quella di mio padre.**

Which books are you reading? The teacher's.

The teacher's → *the ones* of the teacher
2. ANTECEDENT: books (**libri**)
3. GENDER & NUMBER OF ANTECEDENT: **libri** is masculine plural.
4. SELECTION: **quelli**

Quali libri leggi? **Quelli** del professore.

▼▼▼▼▼▼▼▼▼▼▼▼▼▼▼▼▼▼REVIEW▼▼▼▼▼▼▼▼▼▼▼▼▼▼▼▼▼▼

Circle the demonstrative pronouns in the following sentences.
- Draw an arrow from the demonstrative pronoun to its antecedent.
- Indicate if the antecedent is singular (S) or plural (P).
- Fill in the demonstrative pronoun in the Italian sentences.

1. I did not buy that shirt because I like this one.

   ANTECEDENT IN ITALIAN: feminine   S   P

   Non ho comprato quella camicia perchè mi piace _____.

2. These newspapers are more interesting than those.

   ANTECEDENT IN ITALIAN: masculine   S   P

   Questi giornali sono più interesanti di _____.

3. What book are you reading? The one you gave me.

   ANTECEDENT IN ITALIAN: masculine   S   P

   Quale libro stai leggendo? _____ che mi hai regalato.

4. Which films do you prefer? Fellini's (the ones of Fellini).

   ANTECEDENT IN ITALIAN: masculine   S   P

   Quali film preferisci? _____ Fellini.

45. WHAT IS A POSSESSIVE PRONOUN?

A **possessive pronoun** is a word that replaces a noun and indicates the possessor of that noun. Possessive comes from *possess,* to own.

Whose house is that? It's *mine.*

Mine is a pronoun that replaces the words "my house" and shows who possesses the house.

IN ENGLISH
Here is a list of the possessive pronouns.

Singular

1st person		mine
2nd person		yours
3rd person	(masc.)	his
	(fem.)	hers
	(neuter)	its

Plural

1st person	ours
2nd person	yours
3rd person	theirs

Possessive pronouns never change their form, regardless of the thing possessed; they refer only to the possessor.

Is that your house? Yes, it's *mine.*
Are those your keys? Yes, they're *mine.*

> The same possessive pronoun *(mine)* is used, although the objects possessed are different in number *(house* is singular, *keys* is plural).

John's car is blue. *His* is blue.
Mary's car is blue. *Hers* is blue.

> Although the object possessed is the same *(car)*, the possessive pronoun is different because the possessor is different *(John* is masculine singular; *Mary* is feminine singular).

IN ITALIAN
The possessive pronoun refers to the possessor, but, like all Italian pronouns, it must agree in gender and number with its antecedent. Therefore, there are masculine and feminine forms in both the singular and plural. The forms of the possessive pronouns are identical to the forms of the possessive adjective, and they are also preceded by the

definite article. The only difference between the possessive adjectives and the possessive pronouns is that the possessive adjective is followed by the noun it modifies, whereas the possessive pronoun replaces the noun.

> Io leggo le mie riviste; tu leggi **le tue**.
>
> antecedent → fem. pl.   fem. pl.
>
> **Le tue** refers to the possessor (**tu**), but agrees in gender and number with the noun being replaced (**rivisite**).
>
> *I am reading my magazines; you are reading* ***yours***.

> Noi vediamo spesso le nostre sorelle; voi non vedete **le vostre**.
>
> antecedent → fem. pl.   fem. pl.
>
> **Le vostre** refers to the possessor (**voi**), but agrees in gender and number with the noun being replaced (**sorelle**).
>
> *We see our sisters often; you don't see* ***yours***.

For the different forms, use the chart on p. 129 as reference.

▼▼▼▼▼▼▼▼▼▼▼▼▼▼▼▼▼▼REVIEW▼▼▼▼▼▼▼▼▼▼▼▼▼▼▼▼▼

Underline the possessive pronouns in the sentences below.
- Draw an arrow from the possessive pronoun to its antecedent.
- Indicate whether the antecedent is singular (S) or plural (P).
- Fill in the possessive pronoun in the Italian sentences.

1. I won't take your car. I'll take mine.

   ANTECEDENT IN ITALIAN: feminine   S   P

   Non prendo la tua macchina. Prendo _____

2. I'm not going with my little brother. I'm going with hers.

   ANTECEDENT IN ITALIAN: masculine   S   P

   Non vado con il mio fratellino. Vado con _____

3. Our children are fine, thanks, and yours (fam. pl.)?

   ANTECEDENT IN ITALIAN: masculine   S   P

   I nostri bambini stanno bene, grazie, e _____

4. Here is my key; they forgot theirs.

   ANTECEDENT IN ITALIAN: feminine   S   P

   Ecco la mia chiave; hanno dimenticato _____

46. WHAT IS A RELATIVE PRONOUN?

A **relative pronoun** is a word that serves two purposes:

1. As a pronoun it usually stands for a noun or another pronoun previously mentioned. The noun or pronoun referred to is called **the antecedent.**

This is the boy *who* broke the window.
            |
        antecedent

The antecedent is part of the **main clause,** that is, a group of words containing a subject and a verb expressing a complete thought. A main clause can stand alone as a complete sentence.

2. It introduces a **subordinate clause,** that is, a group of words having a subject and verb, but not expressing a complete thought.

     main clause   subordinate clause
This is the boy *who* broke the window.
               subject   verb

["who broke the window" is not a complete sentence]

The above subordinate clause is also called a **relative clause** because it is introduced by the relative pronoun *who.* The relative clause gives us additional information about the antecedent *boy.*

There are also relative pronouns which are used without an expressed antecedent (see p. 183).

Construction of Relative Clauses

IN ENGLISH

Relative clauses are very common. We use them every day without giving much thought as to why and how we construct them. The relative pronoun allows us to combine in a single sentence two thoughts which have a common element.

sentence a   The students passed the exam.
sentence b   The students attended class regularly.

The common element to both sentences is the noun *students. Students* in sentence **a**, the main clause, will be the antecedent. *Students* in sentence **b**, the subordinate clause, will be replaced by the relative pronoun *who* or t*hat.*

relative clause
The students *who* passed the exam attended class regularly.
antecedent   relative pronoun

sentence a   The man was young.
sentence b   We were talking about the man.

The common element to both sentences is the noun *man*. *Man* in sentence a, the main clause, will be the antecedent. *Man* in sentence b, the subordinate clause, will be replaced by the relative pronoun *who(m)* or *that*.

There are three possible ways to combine these two sentences.

1. combined The man *that* we were talking about was young.
antecedent   relative clause

The relative clause "that we were talking *about*" has a dangling preposition (see p. 139).

2. combined   The man we were talking about was young.
antecedent   relative clause

The relative pronoun beginning the relative clause "*who(m)* or *that* we were talking about" can be omitted.

3. combined   The man *about whom* we were talking was young.
antecedent   relative clause

To avoid the dangling preposition, the preposition *(about)* can be placed at the beginning of the clause.

The fact that the relative pronoun can be omitted makes it sometimes difficult to identify relative clauses in English.

IN ITALIAN
As in English, two separate sentences can be combined with a relative pronoun. However, be sure to remember the following two differences:

1. the relative pronoun can never be omitted (as in example 2 above).

2. a preposition cannot be dangling at the end of the relative clause (as in 1 above). It must be placed at the beginning of the clause followed by its object, the relative pronoun (as in example 3 above).

Selection of Relative Pronouns

A relative pronoun can have different functions in the relative clause. It can be subject, direct object, indirect object, or object of a preposition. Since your selection of the relative pronoun will usually depend on its function, we shall study each function separately.

IN ENGLISH
In many cases the selection of a relative pronoun depends not only on its function in the relative clause, but also on whether the antecedent is a "person" (this category includes human beings and live animals) or a "thing" (this category includes objects and ideas).

IN ITALIAN
The main difference between the use of relative pronouns in Italian and English is that, unlike English, where the relative pronoun can sometimes be omitted, the relative pronoun must always be expressed. Also, a relative pronoun is not affected by whether its antecedent is a person or a thing.

Subject of the Relative Clause

IN ENGLISH
There are three relative pronouns that can be used as subjects of a relative clause, depending on whether the relative pronoun refers to a person or to a thing.

"Person"
Who or *that* is used for the subject of the clause.

> She is the only student *who* answers all the time.
> She is the only student *that* answers all the time.
> |
>   antecedent
> *Who* is the subject of *answers. That* is the subject of *answers.*

"Thing"
Which or *that* is used for the subject of the clause.

> This is the book *which* is so popular.
> This is the movie *that* is so popular.
> |
>   antecedent
> *Which* is the subject of *is. That* is the subject of *is.*

IN ITALIAN
There is only one relative pronoun that can be used as subject of a relative clause → **che.**

> È la sola studentessa **che** risponde sempre.
> *She is the only student **who** answers all the time.*
> *She is the only student **that** answers all the time.*

> Questo è il libro **che** è così popolare.
> *This is the book **which** is so popular.*
> *This is the book **that** is so popular.*

Direct Object of the Relative Clause

IN ENGLISH
There are three relative pronouns that can be used as direct objects of a relative clause, depending on whether the relative pronoun refers to a person or a thing. We have indicated relative pronouns in parentheses because they are often omitted.

"Person"
Whom or ***that*** is used as a direct object of a clause.

> This is the student *(whom)* I saw yesterday.
> This is the student *(that)* I saw yesterday.
> |
>   antecedent
> *Whom* is the direct object of *saw. That* is the direct object of *saw.*
> *(I* is the subject of the relative clause.)

"Thing"
Which or ***that*** is used as a direct object of a clause.

> This is the book *(which)* Paul bought.
> This is the book *(that)* Paul bought.
> |
>   antecedent
> *Which* is the direct object of *bought. That* is the direct object of
> *bought. (Paul* is the subject of the relative clause.)

IN ITALIAN
There is only one relative pronoun that can be used as direct object of a relative clause → **che.**

> Questo è lo studente **che** ho visto ieri.
> *This is the student (**that** or **whom**) I saw yesterday.*

Ecco il libro **che** ho comprato.
*Here is the book (**which** or **that**) I bought.*

Indirect Object or Object of a Preposition in the Relative Clause

The relative pronoun as an indirect object and as an object of a preposition involve prepositions. As an indirect object it is the object of the preposition *to* or *for* and as an object of a preposition it is the object of any preposition other than *to* or *for* (see pp. 145-47).

It is difficult to identify the function of a relative pronoun as an indirect object or an object of a preposition because in English a preposition is often placed at the end of the sentence, separated from the relative pronoun to which it is linked. This separation of a preposition from its object is called a **dangling preposition** (see p. 139).

To make it easier for you to identify a relative pronoun as an indirect object or an object of a preposition, you will have to restructure the sentence as follows:

1. place the preposition right after the antecedent

2. reinstate the relative pronoun after the preposition

See the examples under "In English" below.

IN ENGLISH
There are two relative pronouns used as indirect objects and objects of a preposition, depending on whether you are referring to a person or a thing.

"Person"
Whom is used as an indirect object or as an object of a preposition.

Here is the student I was speaking to.
      antecedent   dangling preposition

Spoken English	→	Restructured
Here is the student I was speaking *to*.		Here is the student *to whom* I was speaking.

relative clause
Here is the student *to whom* I was speaking.
      relative pronoun
      indirect object

Here is the student I was talking about.
| |
antecedent   dangling preposition

Spoken English → **Restructured**
Here is the student   Here is the student
I was speaking *about*.   *about whom* I was speaking.

relative clause
Here is the student *about whom* I was speaking.
| |
antecedent   relative pronoun
               object of preposition

"Thing"
Which is used as an indirect object or as an object of a preposition.

Here is the museum he gave the painting to.
| |
antecedent   dangling preposition

Spoken English → **Restructured**
Here is the museum   Here is the museum
he gave the painting *to*. *to which* he gave the painting.

relative clause
Here is the museum *to which* he gave the painting.
| |
antecedent   relative pronoun
               indirect object

This is the book I was speaking about.
| |
antecedent   dangling preposition

Spoken English → **Restructured**
Here is the book   Here is the book
I was speaking *about*.   *about which* I was speaking.

relative clause
This is the book *about which* I was speaking.
| |
antecedent   relative pronoun
               object of preposition

IN ITALIAN
There is only one relative pronoun that can be used as indirect object
or the object of a preposition of a relative clause → **cui**.

> *Here is the student I was speaking to.* **Restructured** →
> *Here is the student **to whom** I was speaking.*
> Ecco lo studente **a cui** parlavo.

*Here is the student I was speaking **about**.* Restructured →
*Here is the student **about whom** I was speaking.*
Ecco lo studente **di cui** parlavo.

*Here is the museum he gave the painting **to**.* Restructured →
*Here is the museum **to which** he gave the painting.*
Ecco il museo **a cui** ha donato il quadro.

*These are the books I was speaking **about**.* Restructured →
*These are the books **about which** I was speaking.*
Questi sono i libri **di cui** parlavo.

Possessive Modifier in the Relative Clause

IN ENGLISH

Whose is the only relative pronoun that can be used as a possessive modifier in a relative clause. Its antecedent is usually a person, but it can be a thing.

Here is the woman *whose* pearls were stolen.
         | |
    antecedent   possessive modifying
    person   *pearls*

Look at the house *whose* roof burned.
         | |
    antecedent   possessive modifying
    thing   *roof*

IN ITALIAN

There is only one relative pronoun that can be used as a possessive modifier → **cui** preceded by a definite article. The definite article must agree in gender and number with the noun it modifies which immediately follows **cui**.

*Here is the woman **whose** pearls were stolen.*
Ecco la donna **le cui** perle sono state rubate.
          | |
      fem. pl.   noun modified → fem. pl.

*Look at the house **whose** roof burned.*
Guarda la casa **il cui** tetto è bruciato.
         | |
     masc. sing.   noun modified → masc. sing.

Summary

The following chart provides a summary of the relative pronouns.

ENGLISH		ITALIAN	
subject		**subject**	
person	*who, that*	person	} **che**
thing	*that, which*	thing	
direct object		**direct object**	
person	*whom, that*	person	} **che**
thing	*that, which*	thing	
indirect object		**direct object**	
person	*to (for) whom*	person	} **a cui**
thing	*to (for) which*	thing	
object of preposition		**object of preposition**	
person	*whom*	person	} preposition + **cui**
thing	*which*	thing	
possessive		**possessive**	
	whose		**il, la i, le + cui**

To find the correct relative pronoun you must go through the following steps.

1. RELATIVE CLAUSE—Find the relative clause. Restructure the English clause if there is a dangling preposition.

2. RELATIVE PRONOUN—Find or add the relative pronoun.

3. ANTECEDENT—Find the antecedent.

4. FUNCTION OF PRONOUN—Establish the function of the relative pronoun in the Italian clause.

   SUBJECT— if the relative pronoun is the subject of the English clause, it will be the subject of the Italian clause → **che**

   DIRECT OBJECT—if the Italian verb takes a direct object → **che**

   INDIRECT OBJECT—if the Italian verb takes an indirect object → **a cui**

   OBJECT OF A PREPOSITION—preposition + **cui**

   POSSESSIVE—definite article + **cui** + noun indicating the person or thing possessed. Identify the gender and number of the person or thing possessed in order to select the corresponding article (**il, la i,** or **le**).

5. SELECTION—Based on the above steps, select the Italian form.

Let us apply these steps to some examples.

*The students **who** attended class regularly passed the exam.*
   1. RELATIVE CLAUSE: who attended class regularly
   2. RELATIVE PRONOUN: who
   3. ANTECEDENT: students
   4. FUNCTION OF RELATIVE PRONOUN: subject of the relative clause
   3. SELECTION: **che**

Gli studenti **che** hanno frequentato regolarmente le lezioni sono stati promossi.

The boys we were talking about were young.
   1. RELATIVE CLAUSE: we were talking about
      Restructured→ about whom we were talking
   2. RELATIVE PRONOUN: whom
   3. ANTECEDENT: the boys
   4. FUNCTION OF RELATIVE PRONOUN IN ITALIAN: object of preposition *about*
   5. SELECTION: **cui**

I ragazzi **di cui** parlavamo erano giovani.

*Dante is a poet **whose** works are well known.*
   1. RELATIVE CLAUSE: whose works are well known
   2. RELATIVE PRONOUN: whose
   3. ANTECEDENT: poet
   4. FUNCTION OF RELATIVE PRONOUN IN ITALIAN: possessive
      ITEM POSSESSED: *works* (**le opere**)
   5. SELECTION: **cui**

Dante è un poeta **le cui** opere sono ben conosciute.

Relative clauses can be difficult to construct and this handbook provides only a simple outline. Refer to your Italian textbook for additional rules.

Relative Pronouns Without Antecedents

There are relative pronouns that do not refer to a specific noun or pronoun within the same sentence. Instead these relative pronouns refer back to a whole idea or to an antecedent that is not expressed.

IN ENGLISH
There are two relative pronouns that may be used without an antecedent: *what* and *which*.

What—does not refer to a specific noun or pronoun.

I don't know *what* happened.
|
no expressed antecedent

Here is *what* I read.
|
no expressed antecedent

Which—refers to a clause, not to a specific noun or pronoun.

You speak many languages, *which* is an asset.
clause   refers to an idea contained in the clause

She didn't do well, *which* is too bad.
clause   refers to an idea contained in the clause

IN ITALIAN
What → **quello che** or **ciò che**—does not refer to a specific noun or pronoun

*I don't know **what** happened.*
Non so **quello che** è successo.
Non so **ciò che** è successo.

*Here is **what** I read.*
Ecco **quello che** ho letto.
Ecco **ciò che** ho letto.

Which → **il che**—refers to a clause, not to a specific noun or pronoun

*You speak many languages, **which** is an asset.*
Parli molte lingue, **il che** è un vantaggio.

Chi is another frequently used relative pronoun without an antecedent. It is the equivalent of the seldom used English expressions *he who, those who,* etc.

Chi studia, impara.
He who studies, learns.
Those who study, learn.

▼▼▼▼▼▼▼▼▼▼▼▼▼▼▼▼▼REVIEW▼▼▼▼▼▼▼▼▼▼▼▼▼▼▼▼▼▼

Underline the relative pronoun in the sentences below.

- Draw an arrow to the antecedent.
- Indicate the function of the relative pronoun: subject (S), direct object (DO), indirect object (IO), object of a preposition (OP), or possessive (P).
- Fill in the relative pronoun in the Italian sentences below.

1. I received the letter that you sent me.

   FUNCTION IN ITALIAN: S   DO   IO   OP   P

   Ho ricevuto la lettera _____ mi ha mandato.

2. That is the woman who speaks Italian.

   FUNCTION IN ITALIAN: S   DO   IO   OP   P

   Questa è la donna _____ parla italiano.

3. Paul is the student I traveled with.

   RESTRUCTURE THE SENTENCE: _____

   FUNCTION IN ITALIAN: S   DO   IO   OP   P

   Paolo è lo studente con _____ ho viaggiato.

4. What he said was a lie.

   _____ ha detto era una bugia.

5. Do you know an Italian writer whose novels are popular in America?

   FUNCTION IN ITALIAN: S   DO   IO   OP   P

   Conosci nessuno scrittore italiano _____ romanzi sono

   popolari in America?

47. WHAT ARE POSITIVE AND NEGATIVE INDEFINITES?

Indefinites are words which refer to persons, things or periods of time that are not specific. Indefinite words can be positive or negative (see **What are Affirmative and Negative Sentences?**, p. 50).

I was hoping *someone* would come, but *nobody* came.
                positive indefinite   negative indefinite

IN ENGLISH
The most common positive indefinites are often paired with their corresponding negative indefinites which are opposite in meaning.

POSITIVE		NEGATIVE
someone, somebody anyone, anybody everyone, everybody	≠	no one, nobody
something anything everything	≠	nothing
some any every	≠	not any, none
some day sometimes always ever	≠	never
somewhere everywhere	≠	nowhere

The negative indefinite words enable us to respond negatively to questions which contain a positive indefinite word.

question   Is *anyone* coming tonight?
answer   *No one.*

question   Do you have *anything* for me?
answer   *Nothing.*

question   Have you *ever* gone to Europe?
answer   *Never.*

English sentences can be made negative in one of two ways:

1. with the word *not* before the main verb .

> I am studying.
> I am *not* studying.

2. with a negative word in any part of the sentence

> *No one* is coming.
> He has *never* seen a movie.

English does not allow **double negatives**; i.e., more than one negative word in a sentence. When a sentence contains the negative word *not,* only a positive indefinite can be used in that sentence.

> I have *nothing*.
> |
>   negative word

> I do not have *anything*.
> | |
>   not   positive indefinite word

> "I do *not* have *nothing*." [incorrect English]
> | |
>   not   negative indefinite word
> This sentence contains a double negative: *not* and *nothing*.

IN ITALIAN
As in English, the positive and negative indefinite negative words exist as pairs of opposites.

POSITIVE		NEGATIVE	
someone, somebody	qualcuno		
anyone, anybody	qualcuno, chiunque	nessuno	*no one, nobody*
everyone, everybody	ognuno, tutti		
something	qualcosa	niente, nulla	*nothing*
anything			
everything	ogni cosa, tutto		
some, any	qualche	nessuno	*not any, none*
every	ogni, tutti		
some day	un giorno		
sometimes	qualche volta	mai	*never, not ever*
always	sempre		
ever	mai		
somewhere	(in, da) qualche parte	(in, da) nessuna	*nowhere*
everywhere	dappertutto	parte	

As in English, the negative indefinites can be used to give negative one-word answers to questions containing positive indefinites.

> **question**   Ha detto **qualcosa**?
> |
>   positive

> **answer**   **Niente**.
> |
>   negative

Did he say anything?
Nothing.

Careful

Contrary to English, double negatives must be used in Italian when a sentence is made negative by the use of **non** *(not)* before the verb. A positive indefinite cannot be used in a negative sentence.

> **Non** ho **niente**.
> | |
>   not   negative indefinite *(nothing)*

> *I do **not** have **anything***.
> | |
>   not   positive indefinite

The following formula for the usage of positive and negative indefinites in English and Italian will help you use them correctly.

> ENGLISH   *not* + verb + positive indefinite or indefinites
> ITALIAN   **non** + verb + negative indefinite or indefinites

> *I do **not** see **anybody***.
> | |
>   not   +   positive indefinite

> **Non** vedo **nessuno**.
> | |
>   **non**   + negative indefinite
> [word-for-word: "*I do **not** see **nobody**"]

Follow these steps to find the Italian equivalent of an English sentence with *not* + an indefinite word:

1. INDEFINITE—Locate the indefinite word in the English sentence.

2. NEGATIVE—From the chart choose the negative indefinite that is the opposite of the English positive indefinite.

3. RESTRUCTURE—Restructure the English sentence using *not* + the negative word chosen under #2 above.

Let us apply the steps outlined above to the following sentences.

*I do **not** want to eat **anything**.*

    1. IDENTIFY THE INDEFINITE: anything
    2. SELECT THE NEGATIVE: nothing
    3. RESTRUCTURE: "I do not want to eat *nothing*"

Non voglio mangiare **niente**.

*I don't (do **not**) know **anyone** here.*

    1. IDENTIFY THE INDEFINITE: anyone
    2. SELECT THE NEGATIVE: no one
    3. RESTRUCTURE: "I don't know *no one* here"

Non conosco nessuno qui.

▼▼▼▼▼▼▼▼▼▼▼▼▼▼▼▼REVIEW▼▼▼▼▼▼▼▼▼▼▼▼▼▼▼▼

Underline the indefinite word or phrase in the following sentences.
- Select the negative word that is the opposite of the English indefinite word.
- Restructure the English sentence using **not** + the negative word chosen above.
- Fill in the negative words in the Italian sentence.

1. I haven't done anything.

    NEGATIVE: _____

    RESTRUCTURE: _____

    Non ho fatto _____

2. John doesn't want to go anywhere this summer.

    NEGATIVE: _____

    RESTRUCTURE: _____

    Giovanni non vuole andare da _____ questa estate.

3. They don't know anyone in Florence.

    NEGATIVE: _____

    RESTRUCTURE: _____

    Non conoscono _____ a Firenze.

▼▼▼▼▼▼▼▼▼ ▼▼REVIEW ▼▼▼ ▼▼▼▼▼▼▼▼▼▼

ANSWER KEY

1. What is a Noun? 1. student, classroom, teacher, question 2. parents, Sicily, year 3. Rome, capital, Italy, city 4. textbook, photograph, Colosseum, cover 5. Monday, day, week 6. horse, Kentucky, Derby 7. Barbara, Andrew, spaghetti, Alfredo 8. kindness, understanding, university 9. Doctor, George, check, bank, corner 10. friend, Bob, sense, humor

2. What is Meant by Gender? I. 1. ? 2. ? 3. M 4. ? 5. F 6. ? 7. M 8. F   II. 1. F 2. M 3. F 4. M 5. F 6. F 7. M 8. F

3. What is Meant by Number? I. 1. P 2. S 3. P 4. P 5. P 6. S 7. S 8. P   II. 1. ? 2. S 3. S 4. ? 5. P 6. ? 7. S 8. ?

4. What are Indefinite and Definite Articles? 1. i 2. le 3. un 4. gli 5. una 6. uno 7. gli 8. un' 9. lo 10. l'

5. What is a Partitive? 1. N 2. C 3. N 4. C 5. C 6. N 7. N 8. C 9. N 10. N

6. What is the Possessive? 1. the poetry of Dante 2. the notebook of the students 3. the bicycle of the girl 4. the boots of Mario 5. the book of the children

7. What is a Verb? 1. purchase 2. were 3. was, to see, struggle, to get out 4. ate, finished, went 5. realized, dreamt

8. What is an Infinitive? I. 1. write 2. be 3. speak 4. have 5. teach, know   II. 1. to do 2. study 3. to learn 4. leave 5. to travel

9. What are Auxiliary Verbs? I. (auxiliary verbs are in parentheses) 1. (is) talking 2. (Did) finish 3. (haven't) seen 4. (would) buy, (don't) have 5. (does) live 6. (were) doing 7. (used to) spend 8. (will) call 9. (may) go 10. (might) have   II. 1. will 2. did 3. ø 4. would 5. used to

10. What is a Subject? 1. Q: What rang? A: The bell. Q: Who ran out? A: The children. 2. Q: Who took the order? A: One waiter. Q: Who brought the food? A: Another. 3. Q: Who voted? A: The first-year students. 4. Q: Who says? A: They. Q: What is a beautiful language? A: Italian. 5. Q: What assumes? A: That. Q: Who is always right? A: I.

11. What is a Pronoun? (antecedents are in parentheses) 1. she (Mary); him (Peter) 2. they (coat, dress) 3. herself (Sofia) 4. we (Paul, I) 5. it (bed)

12. What is a Subject Pronoun? I. 1. they → **loro** 2. you → **tu** 3. I → **io** 4. you → **Loro** 5. we → **noi** 6. he → **lui** 7. you → **Lei** 8. you → **voi** 9. she → **lei** II. 1. ø 2. loro 3. ø 4. loro 5. lei 6. ø

13. What is Meant by Familiar and Formal "You"? 1. Loro 2. tu 3. voi 4. Lei 5. tu 6. voi 7. Lei 8. tu

14. What is a Verb Conjugation? I. STEM: ved- CONJUGATION: scrivo, scrivi, scrive, scriviamo, scrivete, scrivono II. STEM: dorm- CONJUGATION: parto, parti, parte, partiamo, partite, partono

15. What are Affirmative and Negative Sentences? (Words that indicate the negative are in *italics*. Words that would not appear in the Italian negative sentence are found in brackets at the end of the sentence.) 1. We *do not (don't)* want to leave class early. [do] 2. He *did not (didn't)* finish his homework. [did] 3. Teresa *cannot (can't)* spend the summer in Sardinia with us. 4. Robert *did not (didn't)* go to the restaurant with his friends. [did] 5. I am *not* a good student.

16. What are Declarative and Interrogative Sentences? (Words that indicate the interrogative are in *italics*. Words that would not appear in the Italian interrogative sentence are found in brackets at the end of the sentence.) 1. *Did* Richard and Kathy study Italian? [did] 2. *Does* your brother eat a lot? [does] 3. Can his father help us? (inversion) 4. Is Mark a friend of his? (inversion) 5. *Do* the girl's parents speak Italian? [do]

19. What is the Present Tense? 1. reads → **legge** 2. is reading → **legge** 3. does read → **legge**

20. What are Some Equivalents of "To be"? I. 1. ci sono 2. ecco 3. c'è 4. ecco 5. c'è II. 1. avere 2. avere 3. fare 4. stare 5. avere

21. What are the Progressive Tenses? 1. P 2. PG 3. PG 4. P 5. PG

22. What is a Participle? 1. G 2. PP 3. I 4. PP 5. G 6. I 7. G 8. PP

23. What is a Past Tense? IMPERFETTO: was, was checking, was handling, was crying, was, was leaving PASSATO PROSSIMO: went, arrived, ran, dropped, tried, ducked, grabbed, brought, comforted, went

24. What is the Past Perfect? 1. (-1), (-2) bought 2. (-1), (-1), (-2) had gone 3. (-1), (-2) had called 4. (-1), (-2) tried

25. What is the Future Tense? I. 1. study 2. clean 3. leave 4. finish 5. be II. 1. ENGLISH: PF; ITALIAN: PP OR FF 2. ENGLISH: FP; ITALIAN: PP OR FF III. 1. I wonder; be 2. probably; be 3. I wonder; have 4. must; know

26. What is the Future Perfect? 1. (2), (1) FP 2. (1), (2) FP; F 3. (1), (2) FP; F

27. What is the Imperative? I. 1. Study every evening. 2. Let's go to the movies once a week. II. 1. Don't sleep in class. 2. Let's not talk in class.

28. What is the Subjunctive? 1. S 2. S 3. I 4. S 5. S 6.S 7. I 8. S 9. I 10. S

29. What is the Conditional? 1. C; IS 2. PPS; PC 3. I 4. F; F 5. PC 6. C 7. C 8. F; F or P; P 9. PC

30. What is a Reflexive Verb? I. 1. themselves 2. himself 3. yourself 4. yourselves 5. ourselves II. 1. si 2. ci 3. ti 4. mi 5. vi

31. What is Meant by Active and Passive Voice? 1. Michelangelo, Michelanglo, A, PS 2. The bill, (Bob's) parents, P, P 3. The money, the bank, P, PS 4. Everyone, everyone, A, F 5. The spring break, all, P, F

33. What is a Descriptive Adjective? (The noun or pronoun described is in parentheses.) I. 1. popular (soccer) 2. young (woman); crowded (train) 3. tired (we); long (walk) 4. handsome (Bill); dark (suit) 5. whole (story); clear (story) II. 1. leather 2. gold 3. tennis 4. chocolate 5. tomato

34. What is Meant by Comparison of Adjectives? (The noun or pronoun modified is in parentheses.) 1. extremely rich (Italy); AS 2. less intelligent than (he); C- 3. as tall as (Mary); C= 4. the best in (boy); RS+

35. What is a Possessive Adjective? (The noun modified is in parentheses.) 1. my (notebook); S → il mio 2. our (teacher); S → la nostra 3. your (gloves); P → i tuoi 4. their (house); S → la loro 5. his (bicycles); P → le sue

36. What is an Interrogative Adjective? (The noun modified is in parentheses.) 1. How much (time); S → quanto 2. which (car); S → quale 3. what (brand); S → che 4. how many (brothers); P → quanti

37. What is a Demonstrative Adjective? (The noun modified is in parentheses.) 1. that (watch); S; o- → quell' 2. this (magazine); S → questa 3. that (stadium); S; st- → quello 4. these (records); P → questi 5. those (years); P; a- → quegli

38. What is an Adverb? (The word modified is in parentheses.) 1. early (arrived) 2. very (quickly); quickly (learned) 3. too (tired) 4. reasonably (secure) 5. quite (well); well (speaks)

39. What is a Preposition? I. 1. about 2. from, by 3. around 4. contrary to 5. between II. 1. Richard is the boy about whom I was talking. 2. I got the scholarship for which I applied.

40. What is a Conjunction? (The conjunctions to be circled are in parentheses.) 1. Mary (and) Paul; French (or) Italian 2. She did not study (because) she was too tired. 3. (After) the concert is over 4. (so) they could go to Rome 5. (unless) you are too tired

41. What are Objects? 1. Q: We will invite whom? A: our friends, DO 2. Q: The audience watched what? A: the opera, DO; Q: with what? A: enthusiasm, OP 3. Q: The father read what? A: a story, DO; Q: to whom? A: (to) his children, IO 4. Q: Stefano left what? A: a message, DO; Q: for whom? A: (for) his friends, IO; Q: at what? A: the desk, OP

42. What is an Object Pronoun? (The object pronouns to be underlined are in parentheses.) 1. (it) DO, DO, song, S → la 2. (me) OP, OP → me 3. (him) IO, IO → gli 4. (them) DO, IO → loro

43. What is an Interrogative Pronoun? (The interrogative pronouns to be underlined are in parentheses.) 1. (whose) Of whom is it? P→ di chi 2. (who) To whom are you talking? O → a chi 3. (who) Whom did you see last night? O → chi

44. What is a Demonstrative Pronoun? (The demonstrative pronouns to be underlined are in parentheses.) 1.(this one), shirt, S → questa 2. (those), newspapers, P → quelli 3. (the one), book, S → quello 4. (the ones of Fellini), films, P → quelli di

45. What is a Possessive Pronoun? (The possessive pronouns to be underlined are in parentheses.) 1. (mine), car, S → la mia 2. (hers), little brother, S → il suo 3 (yours), children, P → i vostri 4. (theirs), key, S → la loro

46. What is a Relative Pronoun? (The relative pronouns to be underlined are in parentheses.) 1. (that), letter, DO → che 2. (who), woman, S → che 3. Paul is the student with (whom) I traveled, OP → cui 4. (what), ø → ciò (quello) che 5. (whose), writer, P → i cui

47. What are Positive and Negative Indefinites? (The indefinites to be underlined are in parentheses.) 1. (anything), nothing, I have not (haven't) done nothing → niente 2. (anywhere), nowhere, John does not (doesn't) want to go nowhere this summer → nessuna parte 3. (anyone), no one, They do not (don't) know no one in Florence → nessuno

INDEX